Your Year as a Wildly Effective Compliance Officer

Kristy Grant-Hart

Brentham House Publishing Company
Covent Garden

Brentham House Publishing Company
71-75 Shelton Street
Covent Garden
London, WC2H 9JQ

Brentham House Publishing Company books may be purchased for educational, business or sales promotional use.

FIRST EDITION

A CIP Record of this book is available from the British Library.
ISBN: 978-1-7395785-0-3 (soft cover edition)
ISBN: 978-1-7395785-1-0 (electronic edition)

Brentham House
Publishing Company Ltd.
COVENT GARDEN

Contents

For my remarkable sisters, Kelly Wood and Kimberly Black. Together forever in joy, pain, laughter, memories, and the constant gift of being one of the Grant Girls.

Introduction

I was agonizing over what to do. I'd just turned 35, and out of the blue, I had an amazing job offer to be a Chief Compliance Officer. The opportunity was fantastic, but the timing was terrible. I had only been at my current job for a year. I loved my boss and didn't want to disappoint her. She was counting on me.

I lived in London, and back in the States, my father was visibly dying of cancer. Starting a new job would be demanding and time-consuming at a time when every minute counted. My husband, Jonathan, and I were considering starting a family. And the commute from our South London rental to the new job would be brutal — more than an hour each way when the trains were running perfectly. And they never ran perfectly.

As I ruminated on the drawbacks of taking the role, I stopped in a bookstore. I wandered into the advice section and randomly opened a book on success to a page with a picture of a bicycle and the quote, "The best routes are the ones you haven't ridden." I had sudden clarity. I needed to accept the offer. The advice shifted my perspective, supercharging my career and careening me to the place I am today.

The Right Tip at the Right Time

I'll admit it — I love a good popular psychology or self-improvement book. The very best ones contain nuggets that have transformed my life. Many include writing prompts that promote self-reflection or ask the reader (me) to think about applying the lessons or advice to their lives.

The right tip at the right time can change everything. These books offered not only advice, but perspective. They provided the reframing I needed to solve a problem. Some helped me with productivity hacks or tips on being more influential. Others encouraged me to keep going thanks to advice that seemed written just for me.

Many others have a journey-oriented approach. These can be organized chronologically, by topic or life phase. But all have something in common: the hero or heroine (that's you!) faces a challenge, figures out how to surmount it, and undergoes a transformation. The result is that the individual emerges as a brighter and better version of themselves at the end.

In Case We Haven't Met

In case we haven't met, my name is Kristy Grant-Hart, and I love the field of compliance and ethics. Like most in our field, I didn't start my career wanting to be a compliance officer. Instead, I began my career in the entertainment field.

After graduating from UCLA's School of Theater, Film, and Television, I went to work at Paramount Pictures at their famed studio lot in Hollywood. I worked on script development and assisted one of the Vice Presidents. On the side, I did some commercials and television acting, joined the Screen Actors Guild, and produced a television pilot. It was fun. But I craved something more challenging.

And I wanted to travel. Scratch that — I was obsessed with travel. I knew there must be a mentally challenging job that was better remunerated than my gigs in entertainment and paid me to travel. I had a revelation. I could be a lawyer! Lawyers work on international matters, right? Perfection.

I applied to law school and got in. As you'll learn later in the book, I couldn't afford to go full-time, so I worked throughout the day as a legal secretary and went to Loyola Law School, Los Angeles, at night.

After graduating third in my class, I was hired at the international law firm of Gibson, Dunn, & Crutcher. I made a beeline for their white-collar crime defense group, which at the time primarily focused on Foreign Corrupt Practices Act defense. I was delighted. I wanted to travel for work, and this was the ticket (literally at times). I worked on investigations and corporate monitorships that took me all over the US, and to exciting places internationally from Mexico to Germany.

Several years into my practice, Gibson Dunn sent me to live in London to work on a financial crime investigation known as LIBOR on behalf of one of the Swiss banks.

I had a three-year visa to work in London. I was also single and ready to date. I'll never forget the moment I first saw Jonathan's OKCupid profile on my BlackBerry at Heathrow Airport (that takes you back). I wrote to him. He responded. In our case, the cliché "When you know, you know," was true. In less than a year, we were married.

In retrospect, I was already following the advice I would come across in that bookstore. Both my career and my personal life proved my instinct was right. "The best routes are the ones you haven't ridden."

Compliance Calling

Just after our wedding, the LIBOR investigation was finishing up and Gibson Dunn was ready to send me back to my home base in Los Angeles. There was one problem: I'd just married a British man. I wasn't ready to go. I didn't have a British solicitor's license, so litigating in a British court wasn't an option. I went to a recruiter. He said I should go in-house into a role in compliance.

I was torn. I had my heart set on making partner at Gibson Dunn, but if I stayed in London, that road would end. I had never been in-house. At the same time, I had a strong knowledge of anti-bribery, antitrust, and data privacy law. I'd worked on two corporate monitorships, so I knew how corporate compliance programs worked. Compliance seemed like a good match. I'd try.

Shortly thereafter, I was hired to be the Director of Compliance for Europe, the Middle East, and Africa for Carlson Wagonlit Travel. I started their program in EMEA as the first compliance officer they'd ever had in the region. It was a fabulous job. It included an incredible amount of travel. I visited every European capital to give training. I loved it.

About a year later, I was headhunted by NBCUniversal. Their recruiter told me they were searching for the Chief Compliance Officer role at their joint venture with Paramount Pictures called United International Pictures. UIP, as it's known, distributes Paramount and Universal films in 65 countries throughout the world. When I asked why they'd sought me out, they said I was the only person they could find in London with a film background and compliance experience.

As you now know, I took the job. It was an amazing opportunity. I went to movie premieres. I traveled to six continents to do training and perform investigations. The job satisfied my intellectual curiosity, my love of the entertainment industry, and my sense of wanderlust. I should've been totally fulfilled. But there was a problem...

I wanted to run my own business. My previous dream to be a law firm partner was born of a desire to run multiple projects and deal with many different clients in a day. It was entrepreneurial and risky. That isn't the nature of in-house work.

Beyond that, I wanted to write books and be a professional speaker. I couldn't do that at UIP, and their corporate policies meant I never would. After holding my breath and crossing my fingers, I decided to make the leap and start Spark Compliance.

The Big Leap

Spark Compliance was legally registered as a company in July 2015, the day after I turned in my resignation at UIP. I was officially in business on February 1, 2016, after I finished my six-month notice period at UIP. The timing coincided with the publishing of my first book, *How to Be a Wildly Effective Compliance Officer*. The publicity and notoriety that came from the book launched Spark Compliance into success.

In 2017, I joined up with a partner in Los Angeles to offer Spark Compliance services in the US. We grew quickly. As of this writing, Spark Compliance has consultants in London, Los Angeles, New York, Chicago, Silicon Valley, and Amsterdam.

I wrote more books. I began speaking to audiences numbering in the thousands. Around the time the pandemic began, I decided I wanted to be back close to my family in California. Jonathan and I packed up our two rescue dogs and brought them from London to the States. Samuel and Mr. Fox started as L.A. shelter mutts, and they returned to California nearly a decade later. We now live near Los Angeles. Life comes full circle. Again.

The Inspiration for This Book

While this book contains quotes to inspire growth, increase productivity, and develop a positive mindset, it was inspired by a negative review. Actually, it was downright painful. I'm paraphrasing, but the gist of the review was, "How do you become a wildly effective compliance officer? Easy — just be Kristy. That's the only way to do what this book says. If you're not, you'll never be able to implement any of this." OUCH.

That review was humbling and uncomfortable for me. I'd heard from hundreds of readers who benefitted from the book, but I also knew that for some people, the tips and tricks I shared felt out of reach or esoteric.

To make sure people could apply the advice in the book, I began recording hundreds of videos with bite-sized tips on success.

The tips have come from many places. Some I've come up with myself, some I've read in books or magazines, some came from others' experiences, and some I've learned the hard way. The truth is, I've worked hard to internalize and apply every one of these tips. Some come naturally to me, while others require a giant leap outside my comfort zone.

I realized that I'd collected a trove of advice that could be transformed from my videos, magazine columns, and blogs into a singular source of inspiration. This book was born of my desire to create a compendium to help transform compliance officers into in-demand business assets.

Why This Book?

This book is intended to transform your work life over the course of a year. It is structured to take you from where you are today to a more influential, persuasive, and motivated compliance professional a year from now. In other words, the purpose of this book is to help you become an even more Wildly Effective Compliance Officer.

Compliance Programs As a Metaphor for Your Life

The structure of an effective compliance program is a fascinating thing. Policies, procedures, training, investigations, governance, third-party due diligence, incentives, discipline...these elements are important because together, they create a structure that sets you up for success.

I've long believed that the elements of an effective compliance program can apply to our lives as individuals. Not just the work-facing versions of ourselves, but our whole selves. I've been fascinated by the idea that we can use the compliance program structure to make ourselves better and happier humans.

Applying the Elements to Ourselves

As I began to structure this book, I applied our program's elements to our lives. The programmatic elements naturally aligned with a 12-month period, with 12 themes over four quarters. This mirrors our business year. It doesn't require a January 1st start. If you start today, in a year from now, your transformation will be complete.

I've included personal stories relating to each of the 12 periods. Some of these stories made me feel quite vulnerable. But if there's one thing I know about this profession, it's that we've got each other's backs. It's my hope that my openness makes it easier for you to be open with yourself.

Here's where we're going.

Q1

Q1 is the beginning of Your Year as a Wildly Effective Compliance Officer. It's a place for planning and thinking through how you want your year to look. Q1 includes risk assessment, policies, and planning.

Risk Assessment: Risk assessment is the bedrock of an effective compliance program. It tells us where to focus for the greatest impact.

In our personal lives, are we focusing on what creates the greatest impact? Are we assessing risk according to a risk appetite we've consciously chosen? What is the risk of not going after what we want?

Policies: Policies tell our employees what to do so that they behave in a consistent way that benefits the company and ensures that they follow the law.

In our personal lives, what policies have we chosen that govern our decisions? Are we even aware of them? What rules do we choose to live by, and are those rules serving us?

Planning: Planning is critical for an effective compliance program. A reactive program isn't nearly as useful as one that evolves over time to meet the objectives chosen by the compliance officer in conjunction with leadership.

In our personal lives, are we planning for success? Are we considering our risk assessment as we plan our time and activities? Do we have a plan at all?

Q2

Q2 is a time for action. We've finished our risk assessment, reviewed our policies, and we've made our plan. During this quarter, we'll focus on communications, discipline, and third-party management.

Communications: Communications ensure that people know about the compliance program, the Code of Conduct, and the policies and procedures. They reinforce important messages and make our program relatable.

In our personal lives, communication is a critical component of influence and persuasion. Are we communicating as well as we can? What can we do to be better communicators?

Discipline: Consistent and fair discipline is a key component of a mature compliance program. Discipline imposed for misconduct shows the commitment of the company to compliance and ethical behavior. Without discipline, policies and procedures are purely voluntary.

In our personal lives, discipline plays a key role in ensuring we get where we want to go. Where are you applying personal discipline? Is it working?

Third-Party Management: Long-term practitioners know that more than 90% of Foreign Corrupt Practices Act prosecutions involve third parties. Managing third-party risk is critical for a successful compliance program.

In our personal lives, we need to manage the energy we give to third parties — everything outside ourselves. From industry groups to family commitments, are we giving our time and money in ways that create joy and opportunity? Or are we saying yes to others more than we should?

Q3

Q3 is midway through the year. It's the time to ramp up action to get where you're going. During this quarter, we'll focus on training, internal investigations, and incentives.

Training: Training ensures that employees know what they are allowed to do and not do. Training records prove that employees were given the information they needed to perform their jobs in ways acceptable to the company and the regulators.

In our personal lives, are we seeking out opportunities to learn? Are we finding ways to stretch ourselves, whether physically or mentally? Are we choosing new opportunities, even if they take training and commitment?

Internal Investigations: Investigations are critical to finding out whether or not someone has broken the policies, Code of Conduct, or law. Investigations allow us to get to the truth of the matter. We may be dealing with sensitive topics or reticent whistleblowers. The capacity to do a thorough internal investigation is an important skill for compliance officers.

In our personal lives, are we looking inward when situations are uncomfortable to find out what is going on? Are we willing to examine our feelings to get to the root of issues?

Incentives: Incentives show employees that compliance is important to the company. Incentives reward behavior, and giving incentives for behaving in a compliant and ethical way will positively drive company culture.

In our personal lives, are we using incentives as positive reinforcement to get us where we want to go? Or are we solely using punishment and self-criticism? Can we use incentives more effectively?

Q4

In Q4, we're racing toward year-end in a sprint. The year is culminating with the opportunity to take everything we've learned so far to finish strong. During this quarter, we'll focus on monitoring and metrics, reporting, and continuous improvement.

Monitoring and Metrics: Monitoring lets us know where our program is effective and where we have opportunities for improvement. Metrics are concrete ways of measuring the program's successes. They show us trends and allow us to respond in kind.

In our personal lives, are we measuring what is important to us? Do we look for concrete ways to show ourselves where we're doing well, and where we need to improve?

Reporting: Most of us report about our programs to senior leadership and/or the Board of Directors. We report on investigations, new laws, and benchmarking. We report our program's successes and challenges, as well as whether or not we meet our goals and milestones.

In our personal lives, are we telling others about our goals and asking them to hold us accountable? Are we finding ways to hold ourselves accountable to others?

Continuous Improvement: A compliance program is never done. There will always be new laws, technologies, business opportunities, mergers, acquisitions, executives, and changes in the economic cycle to keep our programs evolving. Continuous improvement is required to move the program forward and keep it relevant.

In our personal lives, are we committed to continuous improvement? Are we choosing habits that serve us and bring us closer to the life we want to live?

How to Use This Book

Now for the practical part: this book is divided into four quarters like the fiscal year. Each quarter is divided into three months, and each month contains 20 individual tips, one per workday.

I. The Thought Prompts

At the beginning of each month, there is an introduction to the theme, as well as a thought prompt designed to help you draw connections to your life, foster growth, and trigger change.

For example, during the risk assessment month, you might realize that you're not pushing yourself enough. Perhaps, as a result of your contemplation, you commit to going to drinks after conferences to make connections and step out of your comfort zone. Maybe you sign up for a white water rafting trip to add adventure to your life and conquer a fear.

Or perhaps you see the connection between the two risks — and do both.

During the planning month, you may see the need to set one-, two-, and five-year plans, rather than trying to accomplish everything immediately. Maybe that means turning big abstract goals of "growing in my career" into smaller goals like researching and hiring a top-notch career coach. Or maybe the desire to travel the world becomes a concrete plan to rent a car and drive down the French Riviera.

You'll get great insights by responding to the monthly thought prompts. Maybe you need to have more patience in your process. Maybe you realize how far you've already come. It's more satisfying to take small steps than to go nowhere toward a goal.

II. The Big Win Record

At the end of each week, you'll be asked to write down one win. Writing down your accomplishments can be incredibly beneficial. First, writing elicits ah-ha moments. You'll realize how awesome you are. But more importantly, when you revisit your year-end accomplishments to impress your boss or get that raise, you'll have 52 weeks of reminders about your stellar performance.

If you do nothing else with this book but record your weekly accomplishments, you'll have a phenomenal year. You'll gain an appreciation for your great work and have a concrete record of your accomplishments to turn to when you're feeling down or defeated. Use your Big Win Record to remind yourself of your greatness.

III. 'I'm Gonna Do It' Entries

Along with your Big Win record, every week you'll choose one of the tips to implement in your own life/work. It's one thing to read the tips. It's another to determine how to personalize them to create your year as a Wildly Effective Compliance Officer.

Let's say that you select a tip that suggests you block off your vacation days in your calendar as soon as possible, even if you haven't yet decided where you're going. By psychologically claiming the time away, you're more likely to take it. If you have shared calendars, people will avoid scheduling you the days you've already chosen to be away.

Now it's time to commit to implementing this tip. Open your calendar, and block the days. Congrats! You've executed your commitment to being more effective. Doing this every week will pile success on top of success.

IV. Monthly Reflection Fridays

On the last Friday of each month, you'll have the opportunity to take a break and reflect on your work. Pauses are just as important as action, and by giving yourself a chance to write (perhaps stream of consciousness) about how the thought prompt has informed your month, you'll be set up for success.

V. Quarterly Audits

Audits are important because they tell us what is working, and what presents an opportunity for improvement. That's true in both our programs, and our lives.

At the end of each quarter, you'll reflect on the 12 tips you chose to implement and evaluate three things: whether you completed them, whether they worked for you, and which you want to carry on into the next quarter or year. This evaluation is important because the repetitive acknowledgment of the measures you've taken or want to take will keep you on track.

By the End of the Year...

By the end of the year, you'll have 52 wins, and 52 tasks you've internalized and applied. You'll have four quarterly audits to help you stay on track, and responses to many thought prompts about your goals, strengths, and challenges.

Big picture? Recording your tasks and wins will illuminate where your actions and values are in alignment, and where friction arises. How could you not have a Wildly Effective year?

Let's Get Started!

Are you ready to start your year as a Wildly Effective Compliance Officer? Of course you are! I'm so excited for you. This is going to be fantastic. Let's kick off Q1 with a good old-fashioned risk assessment....

Complete the book, and how could you not have a Wildly Effective year?

Risk Assessment

And so, your year as a Wildly Effective Compliance Officer begins. Q1 is exciting. It's filled with planning and possibilities. It invites visualization and choices that will create the outcomes you desire. It is a time for dreaming and refining your ideas into reality — and a future state that you will wholeheartedly enjoy.

Our themes this month are risk assessment, planning, and policies. Let's start with risk assessment.

Risk Assessment

Every compliance officer knows that a risk assessment is the bedrock of the compliance program. Without a risk assessment, it is impossible to know where to focus your limited resources. These include budget, time, human resources, and technological resources.

Risk assessment should always be done with respect to the risk appetite of the company. You need to know whether the company is conservative or daring in its acceptance of risk.

When you find out what your greatest risks are, it helps to create a mitigation plan so that the risk reduces over time to an acceptable level.

Your risk assessment should be updated regularly or when something substantially changes the risk profile.

Applying the Structure to You

You *could* apply the idea of a risk assessment to yourself by looking at your risky behaviors. But we're not going to ponder the riskiness of staying up late, drinking wine, or not always wearing a seatbelt. Instead, we're going to perform our risk assessment considering the risk of *not living the life* we want to live.

The risk assessment we're focusing on asks us whether we agree with the cliché that it's better to be safe than sorry. I asked myself this question at the beginning of this year and my answer surprised me.

It was January, and I was feeling really burned out. My New Year's resolution was to have more fun. I thought back to a party I'd attended years ago where an acquaintance told me she was learning "to fly" on the aerial silks. I thought it sounded amazing, then put it in the back of my mind.

That memory prompted a realization. Time was moving. If I didn't try aerial classes, I'd never learn the skill. I wouldn't grow in strength and flexibility — at least not in the same way. I'd let myself down by not risking physical discomfort or humiliation to at least *try* this crazy activity. My risk assessment showed me that the risk of *not* trying was far worse than what could happen if I did.

So, I decided to do it. I screwed up all of my courage and went to the "adult class" at the local circus school (real thing!). I signed the general waiver, which, in this case, included fire eating and trapezing.

As I waited for my class to start, I watched with radical intimidation as the 12-year-olds spun down on lengths of fabric from 20 feet in the air.

I almost walked out but willed myself to stay. As soon as class started, I realized I couldn't do anything. Not the climb, not the hanging, and *definitely* not pulling my body up over my head into an inverted handstand position. As the class went on, I sweated, I fell, and I felt invigorated. The next day I felt as if I'd been hit by a bus and run over repeatedly for good measure. Would I go back?

The following week, I chose to return. I was sent off to practice away from the people who knew what they were doing. Eventually, I learned to climb. I got into my first inversion. I did the splits in the air. I hung upside down. Slowly, slowly, slowly...one step forward, two steps back.

Risk Appetite

Now, it's entirely possible that you don't want to learn how to hang from the ceiling. Perhaps that doesn't fall within your risk appetite. No worries — let's see what does. Answer the following question:

On a scale of 1 to 10, with one being "safety is paramount" to 10 being "live on the edge of glory!", how are you living your life today? _____

Now let's check out your ideal risk appetite.

On a scale of 1 to 10, with one being "safety is paramount" to 10 being "live on the edge of glory," how do you want to live your life? ____

If your numbers match, congratulations, and well done! Your desired risk appetite is in sync with the life you're living! If they don't match, consider ways to change your life to be closer to the risk appetite you want.

If you are living a life that is more conservative than you'd like, think of ways to stretch yourself. Take a class, try a new form of exercise, learn a new language, or apply for a scary big job you don't think you'll get.

If you are living a life that is riskier than you're happy with, think about where you can cut back on your risk exposure. Take more time for yourself, say no to requests for your attention, and make plans to reduce things that keep you up at night (*e.g.,* debt or toxic relationships).

Giving Resources to the Things That Matter

The best thing about a risk assessment is that it quantifies the things you need to focus on. In your personal life, this means identifying what's most important to you. A good personal risk assessment will highlight where you should give your resources. These include time, energy, focus, and money.

List activities that make you happy. Some may be work-related, like giving training, speaking before the board, putting together insights for an in-depth report, or traveling internationally. Others will relate to your personal life.

For instance, right now mine would be:

Work-Related:

1. Speaking at conferences or as a keynote.
2. Leading my team in All-Sparkie monthly meetings.
3. Going through Spark Compliance's quarterly financial projects with the CFO.
4. Recording videos for LinkedIn.
5. Meeting with compliance officers to hear about their programs.

Personal:

1. Going to aerial silk classes two or three times per week.
2. Going to concerts or traveling with my husband Jonathan.
3. Walking on the beach or hiking in the hills.
4. Playing video games with my niece and nephew.
5. Hosting family or friends for dinner.

Now it's your turn. Fill in the following:

Work-Related:

1. _____
2. _____
3. _____
4. _____
5. _____

<u>Personal:</u>

1. _____
2. _____
3. _____
4. _____
5. _____

Look at your list, then compare it to your calendar over the past month. How much of your time, money, and energy was spent doing the things that you enjoy most, both at work and in your personal life?

Reducing Risk

If you're like most people, you probably aren't prioritizing the things that make you most happy at work or in your personal life. Other things get in the way. While it's true that you can't always control what happens to you, you *can* prioritize your time by incorporating the things that you enjoy.

Write down ways that you can mitigate the chances of living a life you *don't* want. Find ways to prioritize what you enjoy in work and in life, then stick to the plan.

I can mitigate the risk of not living the life I love by:

_____
_____
_____

Going Forward

Use this period to think about how you spend your time, focus, energy, and money. Think about whether those choices are in alignment with your ideal life. Consider whether these choices are contributing to your overall happiness and the future self you want to be.

Week 1

1. *The key is not to prioritize what is on your schedule, but to schedule your priorities.* — Steven Covey.

Before you agree to requests for your time, consider your most important priorities. Once you've scheduled your deep thinking time, appointments, time with family, and exercise, then you can schedule other people's requests during the remaining hours of your day. You'll end your days feeling much happier and more accomplished if you start them with your priorities.

2. Avoid Distractions

It's been said that if you have more than three priorities, you have none. Prioritize what's most important, and then say no to anything that doesn't require your immediate attention or pulls your focus from what you set out to accomplish. That might mean you turn down more activities and meetings than you expected. That's actually a good sign. It means you're acting in alignment with your priorities. When you resist being pulled away from your commitments, you'll get more done, more efficiently.

3. It's Risky Not to Ask

When you're doing your risk assessments, start by asking the business what they consider to be their biggest risks. It's easy to get caught up in metrics about investigations and data-driven trends. But the people on the ground who face real risks every day provide an informed viewpoint. You can filter their answers through your educated perspective later, but their first-hand knowledge will illuminate risks you can't see from your desk.

4. Capitalize on the Power of a Theme Day

Setting a theme day can boost productivity. Let's say you've got multiple policies to write. Set a day dedicated just to policy writing. Decline meetings and calls that day to the extent possible, or only set meetings related directly to your task. Once you've started, you'll be much more effective because you'll have all the materials you need to complete your tasks at your fingertips. You can have themed training days, metrics days, investigations days, and more.

5. Approach Situations and People with Trust

Make it your default position to trust others. People tend to live up to the expectations of those around them, so approach the employees and leaders at your company with the belief that they want to do the right thing (unless they give you a reason to distrust them). If you lead with trust, people are much more likely to live up to your expectations.

The Big Win

This week

_____

_____

_____

_____

_____

_____

_____

I'm Gonna Do It

The tip I've chosen to implement is number _____.

I'm going to implement it by

_____

_____

_____

_____

_____

_____

_____

Week 2

6. Tout Your Brand in the Background

Many of us have added virtual backgrounds to Teams and Zoom. Instead of using a bland office background, why not try using your compliance and ethics branding for your background? Try posting your logo, colors, and/or your hotline number. Your background is key because people unconsciously look at it for the entirety of your meetings. Take advantage of your background — it's a great space to be seen!

7. Let Those Who Know Let You Know

A great way to get information for your risk assessments and to keep your finger on the pulse of the business is to ask everyone you meet the following question: "What do you think is the biggest compliance risk facing the business?" I've been astounded by what I learned from this question, and you will be, too. By finding out how others define their risks, you expand your understanding of the business, and therefore better formulate plans for managing these risks.

8. Be Persistent About the Resources You Need

It can be disheartening to be turned down if you've asked for resources like additional staff or a technology solution. Although it may be easy to sit back and accept defeat, try asking again during the next budget cycle. Don't be afraid to ask for what you need once, twice, or even three times in a year. The decision-maker is likely to be affected by your continual call for their assistance. They say that the squeaky wheel gets the grease, and it's true. By politely but determinedly asking for what you want, you are more likely to get it, even if it takes longer than you'd prefer.

9. For a Better Tomorrow, Ritualize the End of the Day

Take time at the end of each day to make a checklist of the most important things to do tomorrow. By ritualizing the end of your day, you are more likely to successfully turn your mind away from work to enjoy your home or social life. Additionally, studies have shown that people with checklists get more done and are better able to prioritize the important tasks for the next day.

10. Compliance-Specific Risk Assessments Still Matter

Enterprise risk management and integrated risk management are all the rage these days. While they have their place in viewing risk holistically, don't fall into the trap of thinking that they can replace compliance-specific risk assessments. The DOJ, SEC, French anti-corruption agency, UK Ministry of Justice, OFAC, and many other regulators have stated in their guidance that they still expect a compliance-specific risk assessment. In many cases, mitigation succeeds or fails on a deep-dive bribery or sanctions-related risk assessment. Assess risk in layers that eventually build up to the Enterprise Risk Assessment.

The Big Win

This week

_____

_____

_____

_____

_____

_____

_____

I'm Gonna Do It

The tip I've chosen to implement is number _____.
I'm going to implement it by

_____

_____

_____

_____

_____

_____

_____

Week 3

11. Assess Your Approach to Risk Assessments

Are you using your risk assessments to create your approach to the program? A recent survey of 1,100 compliance officers found that "one in four survey representatives does not have a risk assessment at all, but of those who do have a current risk assessment, 28% don't use the results to inform the rest of the program." Risk assessments *must* be used to inform your plans. From third-party management to planning your training and comms, the risk assessment must inform these choices for you to have an effective program.

12. Carry a Highlighter

One of my favorite efficiency tools is the humble highlighter. Carry them into meetings and have them handy for phone calls. Whenever someone asks you to complete a task, or when you've volunteered for an assignment, write it down and highlight it. Later when you're going back over your notes, you can easily see what you've committed to. This simple technique will help you avoid the embarrassment of forgetting tasks, and help you to turn in work on time without the need for follow up.

13. Delegate the Delegate-able

Sometimes it feels like we have to do everything by ourselves if we want it done correctly. But is that *really* true? Think through your usual day. Is there someone to whom you can send administrative tasks, like scheduling your calls? Is there anyone junior on your team that you can give a stretch project? Even if you have to redo some of the work, if you can save yourself a half hour, that's a half hour to do your higher-value work, which will make you more valuable in the long run.

14. Take a Risk and Talk to Vendors

When conference season arrives, many people avoid making eye contact with vendors in the exhibition hall. Perhaps you're one of them. Even if you're lacking a budget, don't shy away from vendors. You may need their information if you get a new job and new technology or training is needed. Or your company may have an issue that can be solved with someone's product you saw in the exhibit hall. Take names and watch demos so that you're prepared when someone in your company asks if you have a solution.

15. Play Devil's Advocate

If you're going into a high-stakes discussion like a board meeting or a budget session, one way to prepare is by playing devil's advocate. Imagine yourself sitting on the other side of the table. How would you poke holes in your proposal? What questions would you ask? What points would you bring up that might torpedo your request? Once you've considered the other side's point of view, you can come up with ways to counteract or neutralize the attacks. Try putting yourself in the shoes of the person on the other side before the big meeting. You'll be ready to defend yourself and your request, making it more likely to be granted.

The Big Win

This week

_____
_____
_____
_____
_____
_____
_____
_____

I'm Gonna Do It

The tip I've chosen to implement is number _____.
I'm going to implement it by

_____
_____
_____
_____
_____
_____
_____
_____

Week 4

16. Benchmark Your Program Against Regulatory Expectations

Benchmarking your program against industry trends and regulatory expectations is one of the most important things you can do. But how can you benchmark, especially if you don't have a budget for outside program review? Many great resources are coming out of law firms and consulting groups that provide benchmarking information gathered from surveys. This information can often be obtained by simply giving your email address. Places like the Society of Corporate Compliance and Ethics, PwC, Convercent, Spark

Compliance Consulting, and Gibson, Dunn & Crutcher all create materials that will help you to benchmark your program against regulatory expectations and ensure you're meeting best practices.

17. An Apology Can Make You a Better Leader

We all get it wrong sometimes. Maybe we lost our temper with a subordinate or made a joke that in retrospect wasn't funny, or even could've been hurtful. When you've messed up, the value of an apology cannot be overstated. By showing the humility and humanity to admit that you got it wrong, you invite the other person to acknowledge how their actions may have contributed to the issue, or to let go of the hurt feelings and forge a fresh start. Apologizing is hard. But your capacity to demonstrate self-awareness can create greatness in your team.

18. Email Will Not be Checked Periodically

Too many out-of-office autoresponders include a variation of the phrase "I'll be checking email periodically." The word "periodically" is subject to interpretation, and you may be unwittingly giving people permission to feel you aren't living up to your promises. Use your out-of-office autoresponder to state the dates you'll be gone without saying how often you'll be checking email — if ever. That way people won't expect a response, and if they get one, they'll be pleasantly surprised.

19. Know When to Accept the New Job

It's always exciting to receive a job offer, but it's not always easy to know if you should take it. Studies have shown that people are much happier in a new role if they took it because they were excited about the growth opportunities, rather than to get away from their current role. If you're looking to escape rather than to grow, you're less likely to be glad you left. Evaluate whether you're running toward the new job or away from your current one, then act accordingly.

20. Don't Live for Your Alerts

Studies have shown that being interrupted by email can drain your productivity by 25%. Add the proliferation of work chat notifications (Slack, Teams, etc.), and interruptions can be constant. Instead of responding to every ping and flag, check your email only twice per day, and turn off automatic message notifications on your platforms. Turn on Do Not Disturb functionality. Don't bend over backwards to respond to others on their timetable. Focus on your priorities to make yourself a success.

REFLECTION FRIDAY

Use the space below to record any thoughts, feelings, insights, or ideas that arose during the month. You might want to jot down anecdotes from personal relationships, examples from your workday, or anything that you want to internalize and take away from this month.

_____
_____
_____
_____

The Big Win

This week

_____
_____
_____
_____
_____
_____
_____

I'm Gonna Do It

The tip I've chosen to implement is number _____.

I'm going to implement it by

_____

_____

_____

_____

_____

_____

_____

Policies

Policies govern the way we work. Employees are expected to follow the policy or risk "disciplinary actions up to and including termination." Good policies are designed to serve several purposes. These include:

- Setting expectations for how to behave.
- Ensuring consistency throughout the company.
- Creating efficiencies by shortcutting debates about how to do things.
- Protecting employees from making choices that run counter to their best interest or the company's.
- Making sure the company follows the law.

Policies are shortcuts. They create guardrails to help employees succeed. When people follow a policy, they don't have to think about why the policy exists, whether or not it is a good policy, or if they like it. They don't have to consider if they'd prefer it to be different. They just follow it.

Or not — and then face the consequences.

Applying the Structure to You

In your personal life, "policies" are the rules that you have for yourself. They're also the beliefs that guide your choices and the way you live your life. Sometimes we're conscious of our beliefs. Quite often, we are not.

For many years, I had a life coach named Karen Luniw. When I started working with her, I was in my early thirties and wanted to find a spouse. I was frustrated. I was worried that I was too educated, earned too much money as a lawyer, and was generally "too much." As she worked with me, she helped me uncover an unconscious belief that was holding me back: I believed I had to wait to be chosen.

"But that's just the truth!" I argued.

She asked me if I knew anyone who held a different belief. Reluctantly, I said yes, I had friends who believed they could choose their partners, rather than passively waiting. Their empowering and active beliefs shaped their reality. I agreed to try changing my belief, or at least faking it.

Two months later, I met Jonathan. We were engaged and married in less than a year, and as of this writing, we're eleven years married and loving it. Would we have met, fallen in love, and gotten engaged if I hadn't changed my beliefs? I think so. But I don't think it would have been as smooth and fun a process.

By waiting around to be chosen, I was giving away my power, which made me feel needy and insecure. Choosing an empowering belief made me more confident and happier overall, and that confidence improved the whole courtship.

What are your policies?

Think about the policies, rules, and beliefs that run in the background of your life. Carefully consider the beliefs that might be hindering you.

At work, this may be a policy like:

- I'm too old to be a CCO.
- I'm too young to be a CCO.
- I'm not a lawyer, so I'll never be a CCO.
- I don't live in a major city, so I'll never be a CCO.
- If I am promoted, I won't see my kids as much, and I'd be a bad parent, so I won't try to get ahead.
- The economy isn't good enough for me to try to change jobs.
- You can't teach an old dog new tricks — or teach me data

- privacy!

Choose one personal policy that's hindering you:

_____

_____

_____

What policy could replace it? Consider something like:

- Age is just a number. My talent and dedication create opportunities for me, including being a CCO if I choose.
- There are lots of non-lawyers in CCO roles, and I can be one of them.
- Lots of companies have hybrid or remote working environments. The right one will be there for me.
- I am a great parent. Showing my kids the value of hard work, while carving time with them, is not only possible, it's easy for me.
- There are opportunities available in every economy.
- I've learned new things before and I can learn new things again, even if it is uncomfortable.

Choose a new personal policy to replace the one that's hindering you:

_____

_____

_____

Going Forward

As you go through this period, be aware of the policies you've imposed on your life. Where have you made rules for yourself at work, in your personal relationships, with your body/food/exercise, and with your friends?

Where do your policies force you to play small? Where do they limit the possibilities available to you?

When you find a policy or belief that isn't serving you or is causing you damage, find examples of people you admire who are living in accordance with different policies or more expansive beliefs. Then try on a different policy. See how it feels. Practice it for the remainder of this period. Get comfortable. Maybe even become someone else's example.

Policies and beliefs create outcomes. Make sure yours are working for you!

Week 1

1. 'No' Is a Great Teaching Opportunity

Situations that require a no response can be teachable moments. First, explain the reasoning behind your no to the business, and highlight the policy or legal violation that would occur if you allowed the conduct to proceed. The next time the business asks for approval, they will be more likely to think through their policies and the law on their own before approaching you with a request. The result? You'll be able to say yes more often.

2. Squeeze Time, Boost Productivity

Have you ever noticed that you get more done the day before a vacation than during the entire week prior? It's human nature to let work expand to fill the time allotted, so leverage this tendency by deliberately scheduling tight deadlines. Let's say a report is due by 5:00 p.m. Set your alarm for noon, clear your plate of other tasks, and then work as efficiently as possible to meet your deadline. If you commit to a limited schedule, you'll discover that you're twice as likely to finish your work when — or even before — it's due.

3. Find Common Ground

Keep a personal photo in your office or on your phone to help you build rapport or break the ice with colleagues. Sharing pictures of your children, pets, travels, or favorite hobbies creates an instant bond with others who have similar interests. Offering a glimpse into your life can also make you more approachable. It's a way of building trust and increasing accessibility, which in turn boosts the likelihood that people will come to you with problems when they arise.

4. It takes 20 years to build a reputation and five minutes to ruin it.
- *Warren Buffet*

Don't be afraid to remind employees that their reputation tomorrow depends on how they act today. Emphasize that their current choices impact how people feel about them both now and in the future. Collectively, their actions and those of their colleagues determine the reputation of the company, and in turn, the value of its reputation as they move through their careers and onto other jobs.

5. Make Your Intentions Known

When you meet new people in the business, be sure to tell them your positive intentions upfront. Use phrases like, "I'm here to help make sure you understand all of our policies and to be a friend to the business." Stating your intentions immediately puts people at ease and helps set clear expectations. Later, when you live up to these expectations, you'll build trust and foster lasting relationships.

The Big Win

This week

_____
_____
_____
_____
_____
_____
_____

I'm Gonna Do It

The tip I've chosen to implement is number _____.
I'm going to implement it by

_____

_____

_____

_____

_____

_____

_____

Week 2

6. Get the Hotline Number Noticed

We're accustomed to seeing posters in break rooms showing the whistle-blower hotline number. While that's a key location, consider putting the number in multiple places to make it stand out. Why not add it to badge holders or lanyards that people wear around their necks? You could also print it on the edge of a pay slip or put it on a business card that employees can keep on their desks. By putting the number in surprising places, you're more likely to capture employees' attention and increase awareness.

7. Dig Deep for Details

When you're listening to someone report a compliance violation or make a whistle-blower complaint, one of the most important things you can do is ask, "Is there anything else you think I should know?" This open-ended question allows the reporter to consider whether there are additional details they've failed to share because they weren't sure of their relevance. This question can elicit new data or stories, and with more information comes the possibility of greater insight into the case.

8. Be Explicit About Requesting Resources

When requesting resources, be sure to make an explicit business case for their necessity. It's easy to forget that the business may be unaware of the legal requirements or the potential punishments for failure. By being explicit and using metrics, numbers, or examples of best practices from other companies to make your case, you're better poised to get what you need.

9. Preview Big Requests

When you have a big ask, start planting the seeds well before you make an official request. Let's say you want an external compliance program evaluation. Start by casually mentioning to your boss that the new Department of Justice Compliance Program Evaluation guidelines came out, and that program evaluations are a critical aspect. Later in the year, tell your boss about some great potential vendors for a compliance program assessment that you met at a conference. When you finally ask for the software budget, your boss will be primed for your request — making it more likely to be granted.

10. Take Feedback Graciously

When your boss or someone else in the business offers criticism of how you've done your job or run the compliance program, do your best to listen carefully and accept criticism. Many people get defensive when they hear critical feedback, which limits their capacity to learn from it. When we really listen to others, we then can evaluate whether the feedback is useful, and incorporate it to make ourselves and our programs more effective.

The Big Win

This week

_____

_____

_____

_____

_____

_____

_____

_____

I'm Gonna Do It

The tip I've chosen to implement is number _____.

I'm going to implement it by

_____

_____

_____

_____

_____

_____

_____

Week 3

11. Master the Art of Managing Expectations

One of the most important aspects of being a Wildly Effective Compliance Officer is the ability to manage expectations. Prepare people for bad news or for how long it will take to get an answer. For example, if people aren't aware of timelines, they may become resentful. Likewise, if the answer to a request is likely no, calibrate that response early on. The more you can manage expectations, the more likely you are to earn the trust of others.

12. Take Your Cuisine Cues from Locals

When you're training in a new or foreign location, ask the locals to take you to their favorite restaurant. People are proud of their local cuisine and will appreciate the opportunity to show it off to their guests. If you don't ask, you may wind up somewhere generic. Locals know best, and engaging with them over a meal that reflects their culture will likely help you get to know one another in a more meaningful way.

13. Don't Let the Pendulum Swing Too Far

When a crisis arises in the business, it is easy to react with blunt force. Failed controls can require us to act quickly to stop a gap. However, once you've solved the immediate problem, be sure to go back to examine your initial response. Was the response proportionate and should current measures stay in place, or is a lesser response more appropriate going forward? By evaluating the long-term consequences of controls implemented due to one person's actions, you can determine which to keep and which ones to reduce, in turn demonstrating your pro-business attitude and sound judgment.

14. Model Compliant Behavior

When you're pulling together graphics for a slide presentation, it's tempting to pull images or clips directly from the internet without confirming whether or not they're fair use and not copyrighted. Make the extra effort to obtain images and clips legally and legitimately. Credit the source on your slides, and tell others that you obtained the image in compliance with the law. If you're a shining example of compliance even for small issues, you'll prompt others to think twice about their own behavior.

15. Feeling Overwhelmed? Switch Up the Scenery

Going around the block, walking up and down the stairs, or simply moving around the office can shift your perspective and give you breathing room. Switching up the scenery can help you to shift how you're thinking about a problem. As you reduce your anxiety and increase your blood flow, new solutions will likely present themselves.

The Big Win

This week

_____

_____

_____

_____

_____

_____

_____

I'm Gonna Do It

The tip I've chosen to implement is number _____.

I'm going to implement it by

_____

_____

_____

_____

_____

_____

_____

Week 4

16. Create Your Own Social Media Policy

Many compliance officers are uncomfortable using sites like LinkedIn to self-promote or comment on the latest professional news. While being courteous and professional online is always a best practice, social media allows people to connect around the world. Your network can expand rapidly without even leaving your desk. When you do meet people in real life at conferences that you've already connected with virtually, you'll have an instant warm contact instead of a cold introduction.

17. Whistle-Blower Branding Matters

Whistle-blower hotlines go by many names. If you don't care for "Whistle-Blower Hotline," variations like the Ethics Helpline, Speak Up Line, Compliance Line or Team Member Tip Line might be a better fit. Before selecting a hotline name, make sure it reflects your company culture and gets buy-in across the business. Test the name out with people in different regions, or conduct a poll on your internal networking site or intranet. Once you've gathered feedback, then you can select a name that feels organic and easy to use.

18. Remember the Three Rs: Reciprocity, Referrals, and Reinforcement

Have you ever had to tell an eager recruiter that a role just wasn't a good fit? Rather than a flat-out no, try referring a qualified candidate to the recruiters. Perhaps you know someone locally or via LinkedIn who would excel at the job. By nominating someone else for an exciting opportunity, you'll make other people's lives easier while boosting your chances of being contacted in the future. You'll also create goodwill with the candidate referred. After all, highlighting someone else's capacities is a great way to strengthen your network.

19. Nip Carelessness in the Bud

Be sure to stop small indiscretions and policy violations before they become rampant. It's easy to think, "Oh what's the big deal? It's just a small indiscretion." But this train of thought can lead to a normalization throughout the business of violating policies. Small cracks can become big fissures, and people won't know whether the policies really apply. Maintain bright lines and easy-to-follow rules. Not only will it help keep everyone in line, but it will also clarify expectations.

20. Prioritize Deep Work

Taking time for deep work is critical. To perform at your best, you need uninterrupted time to focus on big tasks — especially creative tasks or those requiring extensive drafting. If you're worried that people will need you, let them know that they can call you any time if it's urgent. You're likely not to get any calls, and your productivity will soar.

REFLECTION FRIDAY

Use the space below to record any thoughts, feelings, insights, or ideas that arose during the month. You might want to jot down anecdotes from personal relationships, examples from your workday, or anything that you want to internalize and take away from this month.

_____

_____

_____

_____

The Big Win

This week

_____

_____

_____

_____

_____

_____

_____

I'm Gonna Do It

The tip I've chosen to implement is number ____.
I'm going to implement it by

_____

_____

_____

_____

_____

_____

_____

Planning

You may be wondering why I've left planning until the end of Q1. It's simple — if you haven't evaluated your risk appetite and increased your chances of building a life you love, then you can't plan effectively. If you haven't evaluated your personal policies and the underlying beliefs running your life, then you won't be able to execute your plan effectively.

Setting yourself up for success requires excavating all the deep-seated beliefs about your life that undermine your progress and weaken your foundation. Now that you've identified what's important and uncovered the beliefs that stymie your progress, you're ready. Let's make a plan.

Planning in Compliance

Planning is critical to executing a good compliance program. The most successful compliance programs I've seen have three or five-year plans, one-year plans, and quarterly plans. The initiatives are carefully thought out and broken into milestones with clear goals. Before implementation, the plans are presented to the executive leadership and/or the board so that everyone is in alignment with the vision.

If you need help with compliance program planning, my book *The Wildly Strategic Compliance Officer's Workbook* can help. The book will take you from the beginning of creating a plan for your program through monitoring and execution.

Planning helps to create focus, and focus enables plans to come to fruition. A good plan concentrates your energy on the things that matter. It will help you to complete the activities that improve the culture, enable people to speak up more easily, and please your boss and the board.

Applying the Structure to You

For many people, it's much easier to write a list of goals for work than it is to plan for success in their personal life. The question, "What do you want?" can be the hardest to answer.

It sometimes feels impossible to plan for the life we want. Day-to-day concerns can consume us, especially if we have children at home or are caring for older parents/relatives. Illness can strike, jobs can be lost, and crises can come in quick succession. All of these events make it difficult to focus on a more expansive future. When life feels out of control in the present, or we're just hanging on by a thread at the end of the day, planning for tomorrow goes out the window.

But it shouldn't. Creating a plan can help you find your center and harness the focus you need to prioritize the goals you want to accomplish.

That one time in Ojai

Recently, I attended a women's retreat in the hills of beautiful Ojai, California. On the afternoon of the second day, we were asked to close our eyes and imagine ourselves five years in the future living our perfect day. We then spent ten minutes writing down every detail that came to mind. We were to write in the present tense. So instead of, "I will be in my fancy private office," we would write, "I am in my fancy private office today drinking coffee in the morning."

We were encouraged not to edit ourselves. Any time our inner critic insisted, "That's not possible" or "That's ridiculous, you can't do that," we were to ignore that voice entirely.

Once the ten minutes were up, we read what we wrote to find the themes.

The Themes

I wasn't surprised to see the theme of marriage and family show up. My perfect day had me enjoying breakfast with my sister and planning to spend time with my niece and nephew at my house that weekend at the pool in my backyard. I don't have a pool in my backyard...yet. But it was fun to visit that idea.

Several elements of my vision surprised me. My vision entailed more speaking, writing, and real estate investment management than I do now. I saw myself signing up for a Cirque du Soleil-style workshop where I could watch some of their aerial artists and learn some of their tricks. I also saw Jonathan and I getting dressed up in black tie attire to go out to a charity ball. It was a brilliant and thrilling vision.

Tying it back to today

We were then instructed to look at the themes in our future and tie them to the present. I was delighted to note that I see my sister and her family at least weekly. I entertain in my pool-less but still great backyard all the time. Every day, I continue to write, speak, and invest in real estate while building Spark Compliance. I go to aerial classes two to three times a week. And I've been giving to charities I care about since I had my first job, typically those relating to abused/abandoned dogs and women's health. I was happy to see how much of what future me is doing aligns with my life now.

Getting from here to there

The last step of the exercise was to consider what we needed to do now to get to where we wanted to go. For me, that meant:

- Continuing to focus on seeing my family and strengthening those bonds.
- Focusing on writing and broadening my speaking opportunities.
- Taking real estate investing classes, visiting open houses, staying on Loopnet, and evaluating potential deals.

- Going to aerials consistently, as well as doing strength and cardio exercises to build capacity.
- Engaging more deeply in charitable giving and work that matters to me.

Much of it would be continuing the things I love now. That may seem obvious, but it isn't. By taking steps to expand the things that make my life and work meaningful, I am intentionally planning to become the person I intend to be in the future.

Your Turn

1. Find a quiet place where you'll have a half hour all to yourself. Turn off your phone or leave it in the other room. Get quiet. Then set a timer for ten minutes and write your perfect day five years from now in detail. Use the first person and present tense. Don't edit yourself. Override your inner critic if it starts to complain that you're being unrealistic.

2. Next, identify themes you see and key details. Write about what you're doing now that aligns with who you want to be in the future.

4. Last, focus on what you need to do to go from where you are now to what you want to experience in the future.

Going Forward

As you go through this period, make a plan for incorporating more of what you want in your life. Plan out how you will get from here to there. Once you've made your plan, let go. Trust that you can execute it. And remember that the journey is half the fun. Getting to your goal is great, but traveling the road and becoming who we want to be next can be amazing, too.

Week 1

1. Don't Start from Zero

When you're beginning a daunting new project, do yourself a favor: Don't start from scratch. Count thinking about the project or beginning a plan for it as accomplishing your first task. Check off the first box as soon as you put the plan together. Progress is a great motivator; psychologically, a head start means you're more likely to make a strong finish.

2. Keep a Notebook

The best way to make sure you're keeping important information in one place is to use a notebook. Each day, write the date at the top of a new page and take notes throughout the day while you're on calls and working on projects. That way, you won't have information on various pieces of paper that are easy to lose or misplace. Having one central repository for all of your notes and information will help you stay organized and feel more in control.

3. Prioritize Your Breaks

Schedule time into your day to go to the breakroom, water cooler, lunchroom, or coffee area. Engaging in small talk with employees will help them see you as one of the team. Casual chit-chat also helps your colleagues get comfortable with you. Then, when a serious concern or a compliance-related problem arises, they'll be more likely to find you approachable and come to you.

4. Stories Can Shape Memories

As often as possible, use stories to illustrate your rules or policies. People are much better at remembering stories than rules and laws. The details tend to slip away, while a compelling narrative taps into shared experiences —

which is how we're hard-wired to learn. Stories are also more likely to elicit emotions, making them easier to remember. To help audiences understand and retain key information, find the story in the facts.

5. Remember the Small Stuff

Everyone wants to feel special. By remembering what your colleagues talk about other than work, you make them feel seen and valued. If someone mentions that their child is competing in a sporting event over the weekend, make a note, then ask how it went on Monday. Whether you're following up about someone's vacation or how their check-up at the doctor went, remembering the details of other people's lives shows you care. When you make someone feel special, they'll like you more, too.

The Big Win

This week

_____
_____
_____
_____
_____
_____
_____

I'm Gonna Do It

The tip I've chosen to implement is number ____.
I'm going to implement it by

_____
_____
_____
_____
_____

_____

_____

_____

Week 2

6. Form Useful Habits

Any action repeated over time will become a habit, so carefully assess your daily actions. Identify the actions that propel you forward and commit to them over the long term. A habit can be as simple as showing up on time, which signals to management that you're a committed employee who takes your job seriously. Consider habits that don't serve you as well. If you tend to run late, eliminate this habit, and replace it with one that fosters growth. Small steps can equal big progress, and simple daily decisions can lead you to either fortune or failure.

7. Everyone Starts Somewhere

Have you ever watched someone in the compliance world and thought, "Man, this person knows everything?" If an expert makes you feel insecure, remember that no one was born knowing how to be a compliance officer. The more expertise someone has, the more likely it is that they stretch beyond their comfort zone to achieve a new level of success. But success takes time. Learning is a process. Let inspiration, not insecurity, be what you glean from experts. With more work and even more time, you'll be one of them, too.

8. Short on Time? Steal It

How many times have you squandered a few spare minutes between meetings or while waiting for an appointment to start? Don't let those precious moments go to waste. Keep a list of micro-tasks you can work on in short bursts. Maybe that's returning emails, writing a small section of the new

Code of Conduct, or reading part of that massive report from Information Se-curity. Utilize little bits of time when they arise, and you'll be surprised how those moments add up to many hours, which in turn will boost your overall productivity.

9. Visualize Success

When you go before your major stakeholders for a meeting, pre-plan your desired outcome and imagine it transpiring. Studies show that visualizing the outcome you desire makes the achievement more likely. If this is out of your comfort zone, then start small. Write down one or two specific objectives for your meeting, then rehearse in your mind what those objectives look like. By visualizing small wins, you can start manifesting big successes.

10. Every battle is won before it is fought. - *Sun Tzu*

Keep this profound quote in mind when you consider strategy as it relates to your program. Choose areas of focus and give yourself specific deliverables with timelines. Although you may have to take time to fight fires, focusing on one or two areas where you can have the most impact will make you highly effective.

The Big Win

This week

_____

_____

_____

_____

_____

_____

_____

I'm Gonna Do It

The tip I've chosen to implement is number _____.
I'm going to implement it by

_____

_____

_____

_____

_____

_____

WEEK 3

11. Positively Prepare for Pushback

When you have a big ask, try anticipating the objections you may receive and preparing your responses accordingly. Let's say you want a week off or help from a colleague. Perhaps you know that the week you're requesting off is a busy one, or that your colleague has a full plate. Consider offering concessions. Offer to do a task for your coworker so that she has more bandwidth, or suggest working over a holiday in exchange for a busy week off. By anticipating objections, you're more likely to get an affirmative response.

12. Plan Your Work, Work Your Plan

When there's a major project on the horizon, it's tempting to want to jump in head first. Instead of diving right into a big project, first create a plan, then execute it. Make "plan your work, work your plan," your mantra to help you remember to tackle tasks according to a schedule. The more you work your plan, the more effective you'll be in systematically getting things done.

13. To Get Better Answers, Ask the Right Questions

You've probably seen legal dramas where lawyers object that counsel is leading the witness. But "leading the witness" simply means asking questions that tend to produce the desired answers — and it works in compliance as well as in the courtroom. For example, if you need people to sign the anti-bribery attestation, you might ask, "Do you have any questions before you sign the attestation?" Or, to phrase it differently, "Are there any further questions, and if not, let's get on with signing the attestation." The latter question presupposes the next activity, leading people to act as desired from the outset.

14. Use Statements of Affirmation

When you're in a meeting or leading a training, it's common to move right to your next statement after someone speaks. This might keep things moving, but it's also a brusque approach that fails to acknowledge other participants. Instead of jumping ahead with your next idea, try acknowledging the previous speaker. Statements like, "That's a great thought," "Thank you for that," or, "Building on what Angelica said," will make it obvious that you're listening. You'll not only encourage others to share their perspectives, but your listeners will be more interested in what you have to say next.

15. Don't Ask the Wrong Questions

Too many due diligence questionnaires are cluttered with "nice to know" questions instead of sticking to "need to know." If you're asking for information that won't knock out a third party or contribute to the risk ranking, remove it. Your process will be faster while maintaining a risk-based approach. Your business partners and your third parties will thank you.

The Big Win

This week

_____

_____

_____

_____

_____

_____

_____

I'm Gonna Do It

The tip I've chosen to implement is number ____.

I'm going to implement it by

_____

_____

_____

_____

_____

_____

_____

Week 4

16. Amplify Your Anecdotes by Using the Present Tense

Use the present tense to engage your listeners at a deeper level. Instead of saying, "Last week I got into an argument with Richard about terminating the contract with the third-party," try, "Imagine this: Here I am in the room with Richard, and he begins to raise his voice, all the while getting redder in the face." By speaking in the present tense, you'll evoke a visceral response from your listener. Though most stories are told in the past tense, past events are considered settled and therefore less affecting than situations the brain experiences in the present. Consider this strategy to build a more affecting presentation.

17. Don't Sleep on Succession Planning

Most people want to feel invaluable to their organizations. However, the desire to be indispensable in your current role may lead you to avoid succession planning, which can be counterproductive down the line. Let's say you're ready to be promoted. If you have a succession plan in place, you can easily train your protégé to take over. If you haven't identified a successor, your promotion may be put on hold until a suitable candidate is found. Look for a successor who is ready to step into your shoes — and prepare to pass the baton. Your career will benefit.

18. Big Ask? Timing is Everything

Are you thinking about bouncing in on Monday morning or waiting until Friday afternoon to plan that big budget conversation or ask for a raise? Don't. Research shows that neither choice is optimal. Be strategic instead. The best days to ask for money or help are Wednesday or Thursday, especially in the afternoon. People tend to be focused on their work instead of the weekend, which means you're more likely to get their full attention.

19. Automatically Grow Your Network

Want an easy way to grow your network? Ask a person from each company you've worked for to introduce you to new people at your old workplace. If they've left their job at your previous employer, ask them to introduce you to one of their new colleagues. This will quickly grow your network, which translates into an ability to draw on different sources of inspiration, problem-solve, and benchmark your program.

20. Saying It for the Second Time

When responding to a concern, ask the whistleblower if they've attempted to report before. If they have and the report didn't come to compliance, it's a red flag. This data point is useful in identifying managers that need training or places in the company with a toxic culture. If multiple people have tried to report and failed, you know you've got work to do in supporting a better speak up culture.

REFLECTION FRIDAY

Use the space below to record any thoughts, feelings, insights, or ideas that arose during the month. You might want to jot down anecdotes from personal relationships, examples from your workday, or anything that you want to internalize and take away from this month.

_____

_____

_____

_____

The Big Win

This week

_____

_____

_____

_____

_____

_____

_____

I'm Gonna Do It

The tip I've chosen to implement is number _____.
I'm going to implement it by

_____

_____

_____

_____

_____

_____

_____

Your Quarterly Audit

It's time to reflect on the four tips you chose to implement. This evaluation is important because the repetitive acknowledgment of your goals and actions keeps you on track.

Part 1: EVALUATION

Directions: Write the number of each tip you implemented, and check each box that applies. Some tips might apply across the board, while others only relate to one category.

Tip. No.	Completed Tip	Lead to greater work success	Improved my non-work life	Both

Part 2: REFLECTION

1.   Which tips will you carry through to the next quarter?

_____

_____

_____

2.   Which tips influence your mental space? (positive thinking, achievement, and goal setting)

_____

_____

_____

3.   Which tips changed your physical space? (Your home office, at-work desk, etc.)

_____

_____

_____

4.   Which tips came naturally to you, and which forced you to step out of your comfort zone?

_____

_____

_____

5.   Which is/are part of a larger push toward improvement in one area of your life?

_____

_____

_____

6. Which revealed existing strengths, and which showed areas of improvement? Weaknesses?

_____

_____

_____

7. *Bonus*: Which one are you going to share with others?

_____

_____

_____

Communications

Q2 picks up right where Q1 left off. Now is the time to execute your plan. You're ready to focus on the most important topics from the risk assessment and put your revised policies into place.

This quarter, our topics are communications, third-party management, and discipline.

Communications

Communications are a critical part of a strong compliance program. You may have the best policies in the world, but if they aren't communicated effectively to your employees, they may as well not exist.

Training needs reinforcement, and that's where communications come in.

The tone from the top is impossible to transmit without email, video, posters, blog posts, or other ways to communicate with a dispersed employee base that can stretch across continents.

Done well, creative communications provide entertaining ways to engage your workforce and make Compliance a partner in commerce. Communications offer an opportunity to add personality to the compliance program and build its identity. In short, they are one of your most valuable tools for creating a great program.

Influence, persuasion, and the ability to motivate others are critical skills for people in every profession and walk of life. They are, however, critically important for compliance officers — so much so that I wrote an entire book about them (How to Be a Wildly Effective Compliance Officer).

Applying the Structure to You

Communicating with people who don't share a common way of thinking can be difficult.

I'm surrounded by engineers. All of the men who married into my family have engineering degrees of one sort or another, including my husband, Jonathan. Engineers tend to think linearly and are highly process oriented. They answer questions literally.

I, however, consider myself a creative. My mind is filled with visions of what might be possible. I answer questions in potentialities. In other words, the engineers and I don't think the same way, use language the same way or answer questions in a similar fashion. This can lead to suboptimal communication.

It's not just engineers, though. In my previous roles as a lawyer, Director of Compliance, and Chief Compliance Officer, I dealt with many people who have what I call an "engineer mind." People in audit, information technology, information security, data privacy, manufacturing, and program management often have engineer minds. People drawn to finance and accounting often fall into this group as well. These detail and process-oriented professions allow people with engineer minds to thrive.

Learning to Communicate with Different Types of Thinkers

I admit it — I haven't always been good at communicating with people with engineer minds. This was especially true of those I'd managed at work. For example, I managed an employee I'll call Janine at one of my jobs. If I asked her if she could complete a project by Friday and she felt pressured, she simply said, "No." That made me crazy.

Why did it make me crazy? Because she never offered alternatives that might resolve the issue.

She never said, "I could get it to you on Friday if we move the other project's due date to Tuesday next week," or, "I can get half of it to you Friday and half of it by Monday afternoon." She'd just say no.

If, after I stifled my instinct to scream, I said, "Can you get it to me on Friday if we move the due date of your other project to Tuesday?" she'd say, "Yes."

It took me a long time to understand that she was directly answering the question I asked. If I wanted her to offer alternatives, I needed to respond to "no" with an open-ended question. "Is there anything we can do that would enable you to finish the project on Friday?" is an example.

When Janine was leaving the company, I asked her about my communication. She said it frustrated her to no end when I got irritated with her for saying no. "Why don't you ask me the whole question? Your question wasn't really, 'Can you have it for me by Friday.' Your question was 'What would we need to do to free me up to get the project done on Friday.'" That was a revelation.

From then on, I learned to respond differently. I know now to ask follow-up questions or for ideas about getting to a solution, instead of asking yes or no questions. So far, it's working.

People who make you crazy

Think about three people you have trouble communicating with. I won't make you write down their names in case they open this book! Think about how they talk. Are there trends in how they answer questions? Do they give far too many details and never get to the point? Are they terse? Are they flippant or dismissive? Are they non-committal? Do they withhold information unless you specifically ask for it? Write down any trends you notice.

_____

_____

_____

_____

Now, consider responding to these crazy makers in a way that might create more productive outcomes. Could you talk softer? Be more direct? Ask more specific questions? Ask yes/no questions to get to the point more quickly? Ask more open-ended questions? Write down your thoughts here:

_____

_____

_____

_____

Going Forward

Use this period to notice when someone's communication style is making you frustrated, unhappy, or uncomfortable. Think about how you can be a better communicator, not just with people who you find challenging, but also with your friends and colleagues. Better still, try to improve your communication with people you've just met. The more comfortable you are meeting new people, the easier expanding your network and friendship circle will be.

Week 1

1. Batch What You Can

Do you tackle recurring tasks on a regular basis? Perhaps you write a blurb for the monthly HR or company-wide email newsletter. Maybe you're giving live training on gifts and hospitality to several groups this year, and each one must be tailored to meet the specific needs of the group. If you can batch recurring tasks together, you'll optimize your time and boost efficiency. For instance, take the training slides and amend them at one time, saving each version with titles representing each training group. You'll take advantage of being in the zone while freeing up time later in the year.

2. Yep, You Need to Use Teams/Zoom/Webex

Remember those quaint days back in 2019 when you'd use the phone for business meetings? Sorry, but those days are over. After we all got used to Teams or Zoom, many of us sense that we're missing massive amounts of information when someone isn't on camera. Subtle facial movements help us know what's going on with other people. The perks are many. If you called into a meeting, people could quickly forget you were there. Now? If you take a breath and look like you want to speak, you'll likely be called on and heard. Virtual meetings are here to stay, so make the most of them.

3. To Find a Mentor, Make the First Move

Finding a mentor who is senior to you is a great way to build connections and burnish your skills. But in a world of small compliance teams, many only consisting of one person, finding a mentor is easier said than done. You can start by asking for introductions to people with mentor potential. Perhaps you only know one other person in compliance. No problem. Ask them to set up a group coffee or to introduce you via email to someone else in the field. A specific question will get the ball rolling, and soon you'll have your own network to share.

4. Leave a Comment

If an article in a compliance-related magazine or blog resonates with you, don't be afraid to reach out to the author. Compliance professionals who care enough to write about the profession love hearing about the impact of their stories. If you come across a related article or blog post, send the link to the original author. By reaching out, you'll differentiate yourself. Pretty soon you'll have a new contact, and potentially a new friend.

5. If You Build It, Connections Will Come

The time to develop your network is before you need it. Instead of networking exclusively with other compliance professionals, try to befriend a recruiter specializing in compliance. You can look for one locally, or at an international recruiting agency that places lawyers and other risk-related executives. Then sign up to receive the recruiting company's newsletter, or check in with the recruiter every six months to get updates about your area of the compliance industry. Not only will you stay on top of hiring trends, but you'll also have a contact if you're ever in the market for a new job.

The Big Win

This week

_____

_____

_____

_____

_____

_____

_____

I'm Gonna Do It

The tip I've chosen to implement is number _____.

I'm going to implement it by

_____

_____

_____

_____

_____

_____

_____

WEEK 2

6. With Groups, Go an Inch Wide and a Mile Deep

We all know the importance of networking groups and organizations that promote our industry. But if you join too many groups, you'll feel overwhelmed. Instead of accepting every invitation, write down the groups that you're involved with, then determine which one or two you find most helpful. Commit to the groups you get the most out of, and withdraw formally or informally from the others. By focusing on what benefits you most, you'll deepen relationships and obtain more information than were you to spread yourself thin.

7. Be in the (Virtual) Room Where It Happens

When you're at a virtual conference, it's essential to find a way to make connections with those onscreen. One way to make your presence known is by using the chat box to ask questions or make comments. Other participants will see your name pop up and know you're engaged. If you add value to the conversation, they'll likely remember you — and be grateful for your focus and presence.

8. Stop the Self-Sabotaging Intros

Eliminate any negative qualifiers you use during conversation or in email. Avoid prefacing your ideas with phrases like, "This is probably a dumb question" or "You've probably already thought of this, but..." These phrases negate the power of your suggestions and solutions, so cut them out of your speech.

9. To Master Your Material, Teach

One of the major misconceptions about compliance is that it is hard to explain. There's a well-known quote that suggests if you can't explain a complicated topic in an easy-to-understand way, you don't know it well enough. If you're not sure that you have a handle on a topic, gather material and teach a lesson. Whether that entails leading a training course, performing a webinar for your peers, or presenting at a conference, by the time you're done with the lesson, you'll know your topic inside and out.

10. Test Run Key Comms

When you've got an important company-wide communication going out, be sure to do a test run and get feedback from a small group before hitting send. Once you have a group of trusted readers, ask for specific feedback. Are your communications dry? Overly legalistic? Do they tell people what they really need to know? By actively seeking constructive criticism on your communications, you'll have the chance to elevate and polish them before they hit inboxes.

The Big Win

This week

_____

_____

_____

_____

_____

_____

_____

I'm Gonna Do It

The tip I've chosen to implement is number _____.

I'm going to implement it by

_____
_____
_____
_____
_____
_____
_____

Week 3

11. Prepare Before You Share

If you're speaking on a panel, preparation may seem unnecessary. After all, you're simply going to be asked about your experience, right? While this may be true, it's best to plan out a few stories to illustrate your points. Let's say you're on a panel about effective training. Take the time to recall two or three memorable stories to share. Tease out the themes — if they're funny or cautionary tales, they'll be easier to recall. A little preparation can make a big difference when it comes to panel discussions.

12. Before Meeting in Real Life, Connect Online

Many people get nervous when they go to a conference or networking event. Quell those nerves by looking up the speakers before you attend, then send a LinkedIn message or email to one or more of them telling them you're excited about their presentation. You can also review the list of attendees or vendors. Ask your industry friends if they can introduce you to anyone they know attending the conference. Looking forward to meeting just one other person will make the coffee breaks and cocktail hours less intimidating and more enjoyable.

13. Put Yourself in Their Shoes

When you're preparing to give a presentation or training session, imagine yourself in the audience. If you were listening, would you be entertained? Would you be learning information relevant to your current role? Would you be able to understand what you're being told, and be able to implement it easily? Always think of how you would experience training before putting it out to other people in the business. Chances are if you'd be bored, they will be too. If you would find the training interesting, you're likely on the right path.

14. Set Realistic Expectations

Many of us go to conferences expecting them to be life-changing events. This expectation is often unrealistic and can ruin an otherwise useful experience. Instead of hoping for a major epiphany, go to conferences looking for one or two nuggets of information that you can implement to better your program. If you have a career-altering epiphany, great! But if you don't, you'll still come away with new ideas for program improvements — and you won't be disappointed.

15. Seek Out Virtual Professional Development

What are your options if you have no budget and little time to spend away from the office, but still want to sharpen your skills? Virtual conferences are the way to go. You can attend many of them for free right in your office. Rather than taking the entire day away, you can view multiple sessions, one right after another, featuring terrific speakers. You can interact through Q&A sessions, and in some cases get continuing legal education credit as well. It's an easy and time-saving way to keep growing your knowledge.

The Big Win

This week

_____

_____

_____

_____

_____

_____

_____

I'm Gonna Do It

The tip I've chosen to implement is number ____.
I'm going to implement it by

_____

_____

_____

_____

_____

_____

_____

Week 4

16. Prep Your Panelists

If you're asked to chair a panel at a conference or internal presentation, how can you be sure the content will be interesting? One approach is to plan the first question for each of the panelists, along with an introduction for each. Share the questions and intros with each panelist so they know what to expect, then draft four or five topics to address. This way, each participant will feel heard, and no one panelist will dominate the conversation.

17. Engage Your Audience

If you're chairing a panel, it's your job to keep the discussion moving. Your audience will tune out if one panelist goes off on a tangent or a long-winded monologue that stops others from chiming in. To facilitate a lively discussion, find a moment when there's a break in speech and say, "That's a great perspective. I wonder if any of the other panelists have something to add. Because we have limited time, I'm going to pass the mic." Lastly, try to leave time for questions. The audience will be more engaged if they can participate.

18. DIY Infographics > Wordy Slides

Did you know that 65% of people are visual learners? One way to grab the attention of these folks is to use infographics. Though creating tools like infographics can seem daunting for compliance officers, there are plenty of free tools out there to help you. Canva.com has pre-built infographics templates, and Microsoft PowerPoint or Google Slides have downloadable templates for easy-to-use infographics. By leveraging the full gamut of communication tools, you'll reach different types of learners and improve the efficacy of your presentations.

19. Say Cheers

Don't rush out after meetings or training with the business. Instead, join people for coffee, drinks, lunch, or dinner. Just after you've just presented or led training is the time people are most likely to have questions. Putting yourself in a relaxed environment will permit others to ask you questions without feeling like they need to formally request a meeting.

20. Sticky Notes for Success

When doing an initial document review prior to interviews, keep sticky notes next to you. Make a note and add a sticker wherever you have questions, then go back through your flagged pages prior to the interviews. That way, you'll easily find your follow-up questions without having to search through the documents a second time.

REFLECTION FRIDAY

Use the space below to record any thoughts, feelings, insights, or ideas that arose during the month. You might want to jot down anecdotes from personal relationships, examples from your workday, or anything that you want to internalize and take away from this month.

_____
_____
_____
_____

The Big Win

This week

_____
_____
_____
_____
_____
_____
_____

I'm Gonna Do It

The tip I've chosen to implement is number _____.

I'm going to implement it by

_____
_____
_____
_____
_____

Discipline

E nforcing disciplinary measures is not much fun. Most of us get into this profession because we want to encourage compliant conduct and an ethical culture in the business, not to punish people who do the wrong thing.

But without discipline — also known as consequences — the compliance program would not function. Following policies would be voluntary, and the company could end up in huge regulatory trouble from illegal actions. Retaliation would be the norm. Things would go very badly very quickly.

Discipline should be consistent across the organization. "Institutional justice" frequently scores abysmally in culture surveys. Simply put, this is the idea that a senior executive who adds $5 to his expense report is unlikely to be reprimanded, whereas a retail employee at the same company who steals $5 from the cash register would be fired. Employees need to believe that the company is fair, no matter what their seniority level.

Discipline should also be proportionate to the offense. The company should have many gradations available. From verbal warning to immediate termination, the punishment should fit the crime.

Applying the Structure to You

The word "discipline" doesn't always connote punishment. The word can also be used to connote commitment and consistent effort. Disciplining oneself through concerted effort is both admirable and necessary for achieving big goals. However, self-discipline frequently isn't fun.

I learned the power of discipline when I decided to go to law school. I wanted to go, but I simply couldn't afford it. I could not believe how much it would cost. I used every calculator I could find, and they all came to the same result: I could not afford to go to school full-time under any circumstances, even if I maxed out the student loans. I already had two roommates and was living in a so-so neighborhood in Los Angeles. It wasn't possible.

But I found a way.

Undeterred, I did what my grandfather had done decades before me. I went to law school at night while working full-time. It would take four years instead of three — and that was if I took summer classes as well as the fall and spring semesters.

I was accepted at Loyola Law School, Los Angeles. I worked as a legal secretary at an employment law firm in downtown L.A. from 9 – 5:30, then I went to school from 6:00 – 10:00 Monday through Thursday. Weekends were dedicated to studying. I started reading for the next day's classes during my lunch breaks. I was religious with my schedule. No matter what it took, I was determined to get through law school.

My discipline paid off. I graduated third in my class, and that enabled me to be recruited to the law firm of Gibson Dunn. I joined Gibson's FCPA defense team, which gave me the opportunity to perform in two corporate monitorships. After three years, the firm transferred me to London to work on a financial crime investigation for a Swiss bank. I stayed in London for nearly a decade. I started Spark Compliance there. I got married there. My first day at law school was the launching point for the rest of my life.

What got me through each of those study-filled lunch breaks and Saturdays at the library was a vision of being a successful lawyer. If I could do that, then I'd be able to buy an apartment. I could have a dog. I could do work that I enjoyed much more than the secretarial work I was doing every day. I could join a practice group where I'd be paid to travel. The vision created magnetism toward my future. This enabled the pull that created the discipline that resulted in the reality I wanted.

What do you need to do?

Go back to the planning section of this book. Review your five-year visualization experience. Choose one element from your vision. It can be related to health, relationships, work status, finances, or anything else that makes you happy.

Fill in the following.

1.When it comes to the element of the vision, where are you now?

_____

_____

_____

_____

2. What would it feel like to have achieved or actualized this part of your vision? (really feel into this)

_____

_____

_____

_____

3. What discipline would you need to adopt to reach this vision, and how would you practice it?

_____

_____

_____

_____

4. Is it worth it to you to commit to doing that? _____.

Going Forward

During this period, remember that choosing a repeated action means choosing the result of that action. For instance, if I go to aerial class twice a week, I'll be better at aerials, but also stronger, more flexible, and less prone to mobility issues later in life. If I don't, unless I choose another type of regular exercise, I'll lose strength and flexibility, and be more prone to mobility issues later in life. The actions lead to the results.

Think about discipline in a positive light. Discipline can give you the results you want if you choose your activities with intention. Fix your mind on the outcome, and the willpower to maintain discipline will be easier to find.

WEEK 1

1. Stick To Your Hard Stops

Back-to-back meetings can be very stressful, especially when the person across the table isn't good at managing time. Instead of continually checking the time and feeling anxious, tell the other participants when you need to leave before the meeting starts. A simple, "It's great to be here. Just so you know, I have a hard stop at 5:00," will do. By making others aware of your time limit, you can exit gracefully if the meeting or call goes over.

2. Guard Your Reflection Time

At least once per week, carve out time to plan and think. Be sure to schedule this time as a meeting on your calendar so others don't assume you're available. We produce some of our best work when we take a step back from the tasks at hand. If possible, walk outside during your thinking time, or just stroll around the halls to get your blood moving. Thinking time is incredibly valuable, and guarding it as a regular practice will make you more effective at your job.

3. Monitor Progress

When you have long, ongoing projects with others, time can easily whiz by. If you're managing a project, it can be easy to send an email or request without a specific deadline. To be more effective, whenever possible, include a deadline whenever you send an email. If you make a request without one, it may linger in an inbox in the "will get to it eventually" category. If you say, "Can you get back to me within two weeks, please?" then it's more likely than not the task will be completed on time.

4. For Major Projects, Build in Micro-Deadlines

Many companies assign a project manager to large or complex projects to help create order and keep people on track. You can apply this strategy to your smaller projects to set yourself up for success. At the outset of a project, create a list of to-dos, or micro-steps, necessary to complete your project. Then schedule deadlines for each. By breaking down the project and setting timelines, milestones, and deliverables for each, you'll hold yourself accountable and sail to completion.

5. Give Others Deadlines, Too

When you have long, ongoing projects involving others, it's easy for time to whiz by. If you're managing a project, sending an email or request without a specific deadline is a missed opportunity for accountability. Requests without concrete deadlines may linger in an inbox in the "will get to it someday" category. By adding "Can you get back to me within two weeks please?" the task is much more likely to stay on the radar — and be completed on time.

The Big Win

This week

_____

_____

_____

_____

_____

_____

_____

I'm Gonna Do It

The tip I've chosen to implement is number _____.

I'm going to implement it by

_____

_____

_____

_____

_____

_____

_____

WEEK 2

6. Tough Conversation Coming? Bullet Point It

As compliance officers, difficult conversations are par for the course. Whether it is telling someone they're going to be fired or disciplined, or giving an employee a bad performance review, some days you're the bearer of bad news. In these instances, distill the key pieces of information into three or four bullet points. Then bring the list to the meeting. If the other person melts into tears or starts shouting, you can reference your list to ensure you'll remember the news you need to deliver — and avoid a follow-up later.

7. Happy Birthday to Everyone

Nearly everyone enjoys being recognized on their birthday. When someone tells you their birthday or celebrates it in the office, make a note on your calendar with an annual recurrence. Depending on your relationship with the person, have a card waiting, send an email, or take them to lunch. By remembering their special day, you'll make them feel special and strengthen your relationship.

8. Constraints Breed Creativity

Did you know that one of the best ways to come up with a solution to a difficult problem is by adding more restraints? By setting artificially short deadlines or imposing additional challenges, you may come up with more exciting solutions. What if your budget were cut in half? What if you only had until Wednesday to complete your new Code of Conduct? How would you rise to the occasion? Paradoxically, creativity and innovation arise from restraints. By making your problem bigger or harder, you may improve your outcome.

9. Show Up on Time

It's critically important to be on time as often as possible. Whether it's a teleconference or an in-person meeting, showing up on time immediately signals respect and that you appreciate another person's time. Chronic lateness can make it appear that you don't value others, which is the exact opposite of how you want people to feel during your interactions. If you can, show up a minute or two early. Others will appreciate your courtesy and likely reciprocate in kind.

10. Arrive First, Then Stay Standing

When you've been called into an important meeting, try to arrive first. Claim your seat, then stay standing until others enter the room. If this feels awkward, simply stand while responding to email on your phone. By standing and welcoming the other attendees as they enter the space, you'll send a subtle psychological message that this is your space, and other attendees are also your guests, putting you in a position of power.

The Big Win

This week

_____
_____
_____
_____
_____
_____
_____
_____

I'm Gonna Do It

The tip I've chosen to implement is number _____.

I'm going to implement it by

_____
_____
_____
_____
_____
_____
_____
_____

WEEK 3

11. Your Mother Was Right. Stand Up Straight

Many of us experience a late afternoon slump in both our energy level and our posture. If we're not careful, bad posture can become a habit. Slumping or leaning over can diminish the appearance of power. There's a reason military service members are required to stand up straight. Standing tall communicates strength and self-assuredness. By practicing good posture and standing up straight — or sitting up straight in your chair — you'll exude confidence, which will in turn inspire confidence in others.

12. Get to the "So What?"

When reporting metrics on your program, be sure to ask, "So what?" about your findings. If you report that you trained 96% of people at the company, why is that important? What does it tell us? You need to make sure you report metrics in the context of their importance. If you can answer why the metrics matter, you'll give the reader or audience a deeper understanding of your program's successes.

13. Put Commitments in Writing

People are more likely to follow through when they have a specific way to do so. At the end of training, ask each attendee to commit to one specific task, and identify a timeframe for completion. Get it in writing, then follow up with them. Commitments in writing are much stronger than verbal agreements, and the follow-up offers an opportunity to find out if the person has any questions or issues.

14. Get Email Rage Out of Your System — Then Take the High Road

We've all received an angry, rude, or condescending email and experienced the temptation to respond with equal intensity. Instead of responding immediately, open a blank document in Word. Draft a response that's as colorful as you'd like, then calm down, revise it, take a break, and transfer the text into an email. By permitting yourself to respond emotionally without the chance of the other person reading it, you'll maintain your professionalism even when emotions run high.

15. Create a Confidential Network

Ask three or four of your friends in compliance if they're willing to join an informal network where you can answer each other's questions and benchmark your program. Let each person know that their questions and answers will remain confidential. This way, you have a pre-formed group to help you whenever you need a quick answer, and you can help others get the answers they need in a fast, confidential way.

The Big Win

This week

_____
_____
_____
_____
_____
_____
_____

I'm Gonna Do It

The tip I've chosen to implement is number _____.

I'm going to implement it by

_____
_____
_____
_____
_____
_____
_____

Week 4

16. Celebrate All the Wins

It's easy to move from one task to the next all day long without stopping to feel good about your accomplishments. Most people move from small wins and even large accomplishments to the next task without stopping to celebrate. Take time throughout your day to celebrate your small wins. Checked something off your to-do list? Have a coffee break. Had a positive interaction with a difficult colleague? Tell yourself that you're great at your job, and savor the moment. It doesn't take much to turn an ordinary day into a day of mini-celebrations. You'll enjoy the day more, and find yourself seeking reasons to celebrate.

17. Tomorrow Is Fine

If you're sending an email after hours or on a weekend that doesn't require an immediate response, alleviate the recipient's anxiety by stating that up front. Writing, "This doesn't need an answer tonight," will allow the reader to review the information without the compulsion to respond during off hours. You'll get the information off your chest without placing a burden on the recipient.

18. Follow the Two-Minute Rule

Want a quick way to wipe tasks off your to-do list? Follow the two-minute rule. Any task that will take you less than two minutes should be done as soon as it lands on your list. This will prevent small tasks from adding up, which can be overwhelming. In the time it takes you to write down your less-than-two-minute task, it will be halfway done, freeing up time and clearing headspace so you can move on to the next task.

19. Seek a Technology Treasure Map

Nearly all technology vendors have a product roadmap with new enhancements and planned feature upgrades. Call your software customer representatives and ask them what is coming, then plan for the new innovations. Set aside a budget or adjust your process to account for the new versions. That way, you'll be able to benefit immediately from the upgrades and maximize the bang for your buck.

20: Use Your Cell Phone for Better Presentations

Pictures are worth a thousand words, but it's sometimes hard to find great copyright-free pictures. To create a treasure trove of options, take photos on your phone as you're out and about in the world. Take photographs of stop signs, red flags, buildings, and other objects likely to show up in your training topics. It's an easy way to have great content without copyright concerns.

REFLECTION FRIDAY

Use the space below to record any thoughts, feelings, insights, or ideas that arose during the month. You might want to jot down anecdotes from personal relationships, examples from your workday, or anything that you want to internalize and take away from this month.

_____

_____

_____

_____

The Big Win

This week

_____

_____

_____

_____

_____

_____

_____

I'm Gonna Do It

The tip I've chosen to implement is number _____.

I'm going to implement it by

_____

_____

_____

_____

_____

_____

_____

Third Party Management

Most people in the compliance field know that 90% of Foreign Corrupt Practice Act (FCPA) violations involve the use of a third party. Third parties are necessary for nearly every business. Using intermediaries to do specialized work makes businesses run smoothly and efficiently. As long as the third party acts ethically, they can make the company more profitable and effective.

Ensuring your company is using the right third parties requires good risk-based due diligence. Due diligence helps you to weed out the bad apples early or to catch them later if they slip through the cracks.

It's not easy to keep track of your third parties, especially within a large company. Ideally, you'd focus on each of them, but because our resources are inevitably restrained, a risk-based approach is required for effective management. Greater risk should mean greater scrutiny.

One type of third party reviewed by many organizations is trade associations. Trade associations can create high-risk scenarios from an antitrust perspective. Company attendees may mistakenly share confidential information or make illegal agreements to fix prices or otherwise restrict competition in the market. Knowing that a trade association is legitimate and reputable is critical to ensuring your company doesn't get into trouble.

Applying the Structure to You

The compliance and ethics industry has several trade associations. There are also associations based on geographical location, sector (e.g., manufacturing, defense, pharmaceutical), specialization (e.g., data privacy, trade compliance), and others. There are groups of all sizes.

In addition to the compliance-related groups, there are probably other types of groups that take up time in your personal life. School groups, religious groups, sports teams, your kids' teams/activities, choirs, recreation-based groups, and even book clubs can eat up your time fast — leaving you with little for yourself.

We're lucky to have options, but there's a balance between engagement and burnout. Attending everything likely means you're spreading yourself too thin.

That can be a problem — a big one. I discovered this the hard way.

When I first started Spark Compliance in 2016, I wanted to attend every industry event possible to grow my network. I was already a part of the Society of Corporate Compliance and Ethics, but I wanted more. I joined them all. I went to events dedicated to women in business, people in law, people in consulting, and people in every branch of compliance and ethics. I went to seminars and conferences put on by publications and technology companies in our industry.

Then I started professionally speaking right after my first book came out in 2016. I was lucky because people liked my speeches. My reputation grew, and I was asked to speak at events all over the world. It was awesome for a while. Then tiring. Then exhausting.

By late 2019, I knew I needed to cut back to protect my body and my sanity. I called my best friend from a hotel room in Amsterdam to talk about how crazy my schedule had become. That morning, I had flown overnight from our vacation property in West Virginia to Madrid for client meetings. I'd be in Madrid for less than 48 hours. I would soon return to the States on Thanksgiving morning, then fly back to Europe on Sunday. Clearly, this schedule was not sustainable.

I took my notebook and drew a T-shirt. On the top, I wrote, "Kristy's Farewell Tour 2019." Underneath it, I listed the 25 cities on several continents I'd been to during the previous months. The exhaustion left me in tears.

At that moment, looking at my pencil-drawn T-shirt, I decided to become a jealous protector of my time. I was going to closely evaluate every trip, speaking opportunity, and event to ensure I chose the ones that aligned with my priorities. I wouldn't reflexively say yes anymore. I would be my own gatekeeper.

Conscious Choices

Saying yes to one thing inevitably means saying no to something else, even if that "something else" is sleeping or watching the birds in your backyard. When reframed as a yes to ourselves, saying "no" can be liberating.

Review your calendar over the past month, and write down the events and the group meetings you attended.

_____

_____

_____

_____

_____

_____

_____

Evaluate carefully whether each one was worth your time and whether it served you. Did it bring joy? Were the connections useful or helpful? Were you engaged? When it ended, were you happy that you'd gone?

Take your list and put a star next to the names of those organizations that had meetings that proved useful, and put an X next to those that didn't do much for you. Now cross out every organization with an X next to it. Your job is to withdraw from them or to say no next time they make a request. Remember, "no" is a complete sentence.

Going Forward

During this period, choose to be a jealous protector of your time. Pause before saying yes, especially to activities and meet-ups you don't really want to attend. Practice saying no graciously without making up excuses. A go-to phrase for me is, "Thanks so much for the invitation, it's just not for me. I'm sure it's going to be great though!" Prioritize yourself this month. You're worth it.

Week 1

1. Know the Needs of Your Stakeholders

Scheduling regular time to check in with important stakeholders in your program is crucial for relationship building. Whether it's the president of your region, the CEO, or the head of sales, consistent check-ins give leaders an ongoing opportunity to share information and strategy. The more comfortable they are with you, the more your conversations will build trust. Over the long term, they'll be more likely to approach you with questions or when difficulties arise.

2. When You Must Say No, Rip Off the Bandage

When you have to say no, do so as quickly as possible. Giving a fast response shows the business that you are responsive to its needs and a team player. Nobody likes to hear bad news, but dragging out an unfavorable reply longer than necessary will make the business angry and make you less effective.

3. Write an Agenda, and Stick To It

Always provide a written agenda for meetings or scheduled phone calls. Written agendas do several things. Number one, they keep participants on track so that meetings keep moving. Number two, they help others prepare by providing key information. Lastly, writing an agenda ensures that you remember to hit all important points. Agendas don't take much time, but meetings without agendas can seem to take an eternity.

4. Optimize Your Meeting Times

There is a science to scheduling meetings, and working with it can help you optimize your outcome. Tuesdays, Wednesdays, and Thursdays are the best days for meetings, and mid-morning or mid-afternoon are considered the best time frames. Whether you're calling someone, stopping by, or setting up a formal meeting, avoid meeting right before or after lunch, as people are either getting hungry or in a post-meal slump. Choose mid-week for the best engagement.

5. Create a Compliance Compliment Circle (and say that three times fast)

If you're lucky enough to have a leader who believes in compliance and ethics, be sure to highlight their support publicly. When people feel appreciated, they are more likely to repeat behaviors. In this way, you create a virtuous circle where the leader feels happy to support compliance, and is more likely to continue to do so.

The Big Win

This week

_____

_____

_____

_____

_____

_____

_____

I'm Gonna Do It

The tip I've chosen to implement is number ____.
I'm going to implement it by

_____

_____

_____

_____

_____

_____

_____

Week 2

6. Don't Stoke the Flames of Disagreement

We've all had water cooler conversations where we disagreed with someone else's opinion. When you encounter someone with a different point of view, try finding out more. Make non-judgmental statements and ask questions that neither validate nor contradict their perspective. Try, "That's an interesting point of view," or "I've not thought of it that way before. When did you start to feel this way?" Arguing immediately shuts down the conversation, and while you may not change any minds, at least you won't get entangled in a fight you can't win.

7. Silence Can Be a Power Move

We often feel pressure to respond to emails and messages immediately. We think it demonstrates our control, but sometimes, the power move is to sit on your response. Our silence can communicate that we're contemplative, or that we're busy and important. Instead of defaulting to a quick response, make a conscious choice to wait in some cases. You'll feel more powerful and decisive in your actions.

8. To Diffuse Conflict, Delegate Authority

We've all had to roll out unpopular or cumbersome initiatives to make employees more compliant. To manage pushback, try using "delegated authority." Let's say someone complains about the third-party due diligence process. Instead of defending the process yourself, say that the Board mandated that the company implement the process. You can invoke the designated authority of the CEO, top management, or even the law. By making the situation an extension of the authority delegated to you, you can mitigate any hostility and make the decision more palatable for the complainer.

9. Harness the Power of the Pack

Do you want a magic phrase that will help you in your day-to-day life? Of course you do. Start with, "What most people do..." followed by the action you'd like the other person to take. The reason? For all our intellectual abilities, humans remain social animals. We're wired to follow the pack. If we hear that others are doing something, we tend to follow suit. These magic words are an accessible persuasive technique. After all, most Wildly Effective Compliance Officers are deft at using speech to get what they want.

10. Apply the Same Rules to All

Never forget that whenever you're dealing with a difficult investigation, other people are watching. If a senior leader is in trouble, you can be sure others know about it. Likewise, if junior staff have made mistakes, their peers likely know about it too. Many companies underestimate the power of institutional justice. If you treat lower-level employees who make ethical slip-ups the same way that you treat senior people with similar issues, you create trust. If you don't, people will notice, and that will undermine the integrity of your program.

The Big Win

This week

_____

_____

_____

_____

_____

_____

_____

I'm Gonna Do It

The tip I've chosen to implement is number _____.

I'm going to implement it by

_____

_____

_____

_____

_____

_____

_____

Week 3

11. New Law on the Books? Call in the Legal Cavalry

When you find out about a new law that may affect your business, call your local law firm before diving into research. You may be able to bring in specialists to perform a free educational session about the law or gain access to articles that inform clients about the law and its applications. By starting with lawyers, you'll harness the power of their expertise, rather than going down a research rabbit hole. As a bonus, many law firms give out this information for free so that you'll be more likely to hire them if a problem does arise. This strategy is a win/win.

12. Set Yourself Up for Successful Collaborations

When dealing with other functions such as Human Resources or Internal Audit, try asking the head of the function a simple question: "How do you think we could work together more effectively?" This open-ended question elicits feedback that can foster collaboration and defuse any potential turf wars. Seek advice on how to solve problems instead of festering in your own camp. By proactively engaging across functions, you'll collaborate more effectively.

13. Use Focus Groups for Training Follow-up

It's sometimes difficult to evaluate the quality of the training you've assigned, especially if you wrote it or created it. Instead of assuming it was good or bad, ask follow-up questions and talk with a select group of participants about their experience. By doing so, you can measure knowledge and effectiveness. We need training to be effective, not simply completed.

14. Be Strategic in a Crisis

When you face a crisis or receive bad news, think carefully about who you need to tell, and in what order. The CEO, the Board, General Counsel, or all three? People can be very territorial about information, so make a strategic decision about whom to tell first. Meanwhile, devise a plan about how best to manage the problem. That way, when you come bearing bad news, you can quickly assure others you've got the situation under control by sharing your plan.

15. Talk Less, Listen More

When you're having a conversation with someone in the business, try to talk 30% of the time and listen 70% of the time. When you pay close attention and really hone in on what another person is saying, you build more effective relationships. When people feel heard, they are primed to appreciate you and take your advice.

The Big Win

This week

I'm Gonna Do It

The tip I've chosen to implement is number _____.
I'm going to implement it by

Week 4

16. Reiterate Responsibilities

When you're running a meeting in person or over the phone, don't forget to write down all of the tasks assigned, both to you and to others. Then, at the end of the call, repeat the tasks assigned right before you hang up. In doing so, you'll ensure that everyone knows what is due from them, and you'll remind yourself of your own duties. If you've overlooked anything, you'll find out immediately, which can help you avoid consternation later.

17. Three Is the Magic Number

When you're trying to get a new budget item approved, be sure to offer your boss three options. Let's say you need to have a risk assessment performed. Perhaps three different vendors have different prices, or your favorite vendor can give you three options at varying levels of service, depending on their scope. Some sales teams call this a "good, better, best" model. People value feeling in control and having choices. By offering three options, one will likely get a yes. If you come with a single option, chances are higher you'll get a no.

18. Reframe Honest Feedback

Most managers find it difficult to give employee reviews. Whether it's the annual review or a review on a small project, we often want to spare our employees' feelings. Instead, try thinking of negative feedback as constructive criticism. You've invested the time and energy to help your employees improve their work product or behavior. Candid, concrete feedback is the necessary first step toward growth. If you withhold constructive criticism, you're doing a disservice to your employee — and to yourself. Face your employees with candor. You owe it to both of you.

19. Set the Bar High

We tend to live up to the expectations others set for us, and managers should expect the best from their teams. If you're a manager, express confidence in your team members' ability to excel. You'll help them cultivate a vision of their success. Consciously communicating that the bar is set high increases the chance they'll clear it. Ultimately, it's to your benefit: the success of your team members is your success, too.

20: Be Both a Mentor and Mentee

People should both be and have a mentor. No matter what stage you are at in your career, there will always be those who can learn from you. And even when you're at the pinnacle of your career, you can still evolve and grow your skills set by finding a mentor who has accomplished things you haven't. Commit to always being and having a mentor.

REFLECTION FRIDAY

Use the space below to record any thoughts, feelings, insights, or ideas that arose during the month. You might want to jot down anecdotes from personal relationships, examples from your workday, or anything that you want to internalize and take away from this month.

_____
_____
_____
_____

The Big Win

This week

_____
_____
_____
_____
_____
_____
_____

I'm Gonna Do It

The tip I've chosen to implement is number _____.
I'm going to implement it by

_____
_____
_____
_____
_____

_____

_____

Your Quarterly Audit

t's time to reflect on the four tips you chose to implement. This evaluation is important because the repetitive acknowledgment of your goals and actions keeps you on track.

Part 1: EVALUATION

Directions: Write the number of each tip you implemented, and check each box that applies. Some tips might apply across the board, while others only relate to one category.

Tip. No.	Completed Tip	Lead to greater work success	Improved my non-work life	Both

Part 2: REFLECTION

1.   Which tips will you carry through to the next quarter?

_____

_____

_____

2.   Which tips influence your mental space? (positive thinking, achievement, and goal setting)

_____

_____

_____

3.   Which tips changed your physical space? (Your home office, at-work desk, etc.)

_____

_____

_____

4.   Which tips came naturally to you, and which forced you to step out of your comfort zone?

_____

_____

_____

5.   Which is/are part of a larger push toward improvement in one area of your life?

_____

_____

_____

6. Which revealed existing strengths, and which showed areas of improvement? Weaknesses?

_____

_____

_____

7. *Bonus*: Which one are you going to share with others?

_____

_____

_____

Training

I t's mid-way through your year as a Wildly Effective Compliance Officer. Congratulate yourself on how far you've come! You've been tracking your wins and accomplishments, focusing on incorporating new habits and techniques from the tips, and executing your plan with aplomb. Well done!

In Q3, we're going to tackle three great topics, namely training, investigations, and incentives.

Training

Training is where almost every employee interacts directly with the compliance program. Whether eLearning, in-person, via webinar, or microlearning, training is a critical element of ensuring people know what they need to know to follow the law and the company's policies.

There is a never-ending demand for creativity when it comes to training. Dull and generic training is meaningless and won't have the desired effect of changing behavior. If training isn't engaging, people won't learn, and your time and theirs will be wasted.

Gamification (like Spark's training game, Compliance Competitor), scenario-based learning, and complex situations make for much better training than the standard off-the-shelf eLearning.

Training is meant to create patterns of behavior. It also allows the company to hold employees to account for violations of the Code or policies. If someone isn't trained on a topic, it's unreasonable to expect them to know what to do. Through training, we can ensure consistent behavior and a common understanding of the rules.

Applying the Structure to You

Training can take many forms. People train for competitions to become better athletes. Education can be considered training when it requires repeated exercises to ensure that knowledge has been acquired.

Like discipline, people sometimes shy away from training because it requires effort and commitment. But we can't become bigger or broader without identifying our areas of growth and training to improve them.

Committing to training can be scary because it's human nature to keep the status quo. It can threaten our ego and our sense of safety to cross over into new paradigms or behaviors. But it can also be freeing.

In January a few years ago, I was out at the pub with my work colleague Keely. She was regaling me with tales of the marathon she'd just completed. My mind jumped back to me at age 20, moving in the crowd with the Road Runners club in Los Angeles training for the LA marathon. I saw myself nearly falling over with pain in my knee. The orthopedic doctor at UCLA told me I could choose running, or I could choose dancing, skiing, bodyboarding, and gymnastics. I chose the latter. My running days were over, along with my marathon goal.

The memory of searing pain in my knee was running through my head as Keely told me that she'd completed an overnight walking marathon in support of Cancer UK. She'd trained for several months. She described foot injuries and all sorts of challenges, but also how much fun she had, and the pride she felt when she crossed the finish line,

I was intrigued. I looked up the date of the next Cancer UK overnight walking marathon. It was September 22nd – the day after my 40th birthday. I decided it was a sign. I had nine months to train. It was a huge commitment. To be totally honest, I really didn't think I could do it, but I figured there was no harm in signing up.

Jonathan decided to join me in training. The next weekend, we contended with the ice and snow along the canal path as we trekked a full three miles. I realized that three miles was 23.2 miles shy of a marathon. My heart sank.

For the next nine months, every Saturday morning, Jonathan and I went on a walk. We went further and longer each weekend. I walked three miles every other day during the rest of the week to keep up my training. By June, we were getting up at 5:00 a.m. on Saturdays to beat the heat and the crowds on the pathways. We were proud to be up to 13 miles.

By August, we were into the longest training walk we would do — a 23-mile trek. It took hours. I was beginning to think I would make it.

The day after my 40th birthday, I donned my gear, took the Tube (subway) to the Green Park stop, and pinned on my bib. The race was in support of cancer research and on the back of my bib I wrote, "This is for my Dad." See, my Dad had died four years earlier of metastasized prostate cancer. This training journey wasn't just for me, but also for him.

Jonathan and I waited for the 10:00 p.m. starting signal. There were thousands of people with us. We quickly hit our stride. The marathon trail snaked through London's best landmarks. We walked across Tower Bridge and through the city center. At the 8-mile mark, people who hadn't trained began dropping like flies, crawling to the Tube station to go home. We marched on, grateful for our extensive training regime.

The night wore on. We walked past nightclubs and women tottering in 5-inch heels with their boyfriends. At 4:00 a.m., we went past Buckingham Palace. The quiet at that time of the morning was incredible. It was as if London itself was cheering us on with the birdsong from the trees.

There was a sign at the last water stop at mile 23 that said, "Do not sit down!" It was a warning — you'll probably not get up again if you do. Your legs may seize. Jonathan and I walked on. At mile 24, it started to rain. We were not going to give up, not when we'd come so far. Nearly seven hours after we'd started, we crossed the finish line and got our congratulatory medals, followed by a giant English breakfast and a very long nap.

There is no way we could have completed the marathon without all of the training. I accomplished something I genuinely didn't believe I could do. I chose to follow the training plan to the letter — heck, I'm a compliance officer, it's in my DNA to follow instructions.

Nothing beats surprising yourself by completing something you don't think is possible.

What do you want to train to do?

Think about an activity you've always wanted to try or a subject that you've always wanted to learn. Write down five choices. Look for a variety. Mine would include becoming semi-fluent in Spanish, learning to surf, and having a greater understanding of export trade compliance.

1. _____
2. _____
3. _____
4. _____
5. _____

Now choose one to pursue. Find a training plan. Maybe that means taking lessons once or twice a week. Find a mentor or a class. You can do this!

Going Forward

During this period, look for opportunities to get better at things you like to do. Make a formal training plan with a goal so you can build momentum toward accomplishment. Training will increase your confidence and bravery. It's worth it.

Week 1

1. Be an Introducer

A simple way to show that you're important and in high demand at work is to make useful introductions. When you're talking to people, learn about their goals and interests. If you find that someone in IT loves the same sports team as someone in Legal, make an introduction using this detail. If you find someone in the US office who has always wanted to visit Thailand, introduce them to your contact in the Thai office. Introducers benefit from knowing more people in the company, leading to greater acceptance, and greater esteem.

2. Put it in Writing

How many times have you finished a conversation with someone thinking you're on the same page, only to find out weeks or months later that their recollection of events differs, or worse yet, they don't remember the conversation at all? Whenever you have an important conversation that involves decision-making or strategy, be sure to capture the conversation in writing. Your note can be brief. Simply write, "Thanks so much for the meeting. We decided…" It will protect you in the future if there are conflicting memories of what happened.

3. Keep Private Matters Private

If you're a busy compliance professional, you may need to work in many places — in the air, at the train station, at home, and maybe even while waiting for meetings at someone's office. If you're outside your own space, be extra cautious about privacy. Take proactive steps to ensure strangers can't see your screen, read your documents, or listen in on your calls. Get a privacy screen for your laptop, bring post-it notes to cover people's names, and resolve never to talk about confidential matters in public. You don't want to be reported to compliance for violating confidentiality rules!

4. Branding Isn't Just for the Marketing Department

Establishing a brand for the compliance function within your organization can elevate your department. First, select words that resonate and consider developing a slogan. Are you primarily a helper? A police officer? A friend? All of the above? Find a phrase that reflects your department's image and values. Visual consistency is important, too: use colors, fonts, pictures, or a logo to portray the compliance program as a cohesive whole. A clear brand can communicate your values, and train people to expect consistency from any function.

5. Don't Divulge Details Unless Necessary

When you need to tell the business about a new law or regulation, provide minimal details. The business only needs to know how they can help you be successful, and how they can remain in compliance with the law. For example, if the business needs to post a new data privacy notice, they don't need every detail about the new regulation. Instead, simply tell them what you need. If they want details about the law, they can ask for clarification.

The Big Win

This week

_____

_____

_____

_____

_____

_____

_____

I'm Gonna Do It

The tip I've chosen to implement is number _____.

I'm going to implement it by

Week 2

6. Learn the Language of Business

Ever wish you could talk business more fluently? Why not take a basic accounting or business class? Check out online seminars, community college classes, or read a book that breaks down financial terminology. The more fluent you become in the language of business, the more effectively you can communicate with the business on their terms. Speaking someone's language makes them more likely to include you — and you'll feel more like one of the team.

7. Check-ins = Trust and Comfort

If you have a long-term project, be sure to check in with your manager at least once every two weeks to let them know you're on track. Sending a simple email or verbally confirming that things are going well gives your manager faith that you're handling things correctly and that they can trust you to deliver on time. Check-ins can make a huge difference in the manager's comfort level, which can be a big career advantage.

8. Let Me Tell You About It

Be sure to include local stories and examples in your live training whenever possible. Studies show that people internalize and identify with stories the most when they feature a person like themselves. Try to use examples from the city or country the trainees are from, or use a story featuring a company in the same city, country, region, or industry as the people in the room. They'll be much more likely to remember the training when it feels personalized for them.

9. Images Can Speak Volumes

In training or presentations, keep the text on your slides to a minimum. Graphics and pictures are preferable to wordy slides. Reserve text to make your point or jog your memory about a key idea, but use as few words as possible. People are far more likely to listen to you if they aren't busy reading your text-heavy slides.

10. Use the 5/5/5 Rule

Stress can throw us out of whack, making it hard to keep issues in perspective. The next time you feel overwhelmed, try using the 5/5/5 rule. Ask yourself if the current problem will still seem as big in five days, in five months, and in five years. If not, is it really a big problem? Or is it a big problem that, when dealt with, won't persist, or affect you over the long term? Look at the big picture, and many problems instantly become more manageable.

The Big Win

This week

_____

_____

_____

_____

_____

_____

_____

I'm Gonna Do It

The tip I've chosen to implement is number ____.

I'm going to implement it by

_____

_____

_____

_____

_____

_____

_____

Week 3

11. Bring Bribery Home

If you're performing anti-bribery training, consider using Transparency International's Corruption Perceptions Index (CPI). Ask trainees to guess where their country falls compared to other countries on the list where the company operates or sells its products. People love hearing about their own country, and it puts their risk in a global context.

12. A Fabulous New Training Analytics Idea

Regulators around the world are raising the bar for compliance officers by requiring them to show how effective their training is. One way to increase efficacy is by asking participants how confident they are in their responses before revealing the answers. If people are highly confident about incorrect answers, they probably need more training. Tracking this new metric will help reveal which training needs to be repeated, and what lessons are already confidently, and correctly, understood.

13. Stop Skipping Slides

Many presentations suffer from a common problem: cramped, text-heavy slides. If you have lots to share, putting tons of information in your deck can be comforting while you're preparing. But when you're presenting, you may need to skip slides to get through all the material, which leaves the audience frustrated and you flustered. Instead of rushing through your deck, include detailed information in an appendix. You'll optimize your presentation while still providing your audience with all the necessary information.

14. Be Your Own Best Friend

When faced with a particularly challenging problem, we can become paralyzed. One way to get through a difficult situation is by imagining that your best friend has come to you seeking counsel over the issue. Really imagine yourself giving advice. What would you tell your bestie? When you internalize your response to a friend, you'll frequently find the answer you need yourself.

15. Change the Page

People like to feel like they're on the same page, but those pages may be different sizes. In the US and Canada, letter-sized paper (8.5 by 11 inches) is traditionally used, while in nearly every other country in the world, A4 is the standard size. Pay attention to paper size when you're sending materials internationally. Changing the size for the recipient shows respect and consideration, making you an international ally.

The Big Win

This week

_____

_____

_____

_____

_____

_____
_____
_____

I'm Gonna Do It

The tip I've chosen to implement is number _____.

I'm going to implement it by

_____
_____
_____
_____
_____
_____
_____

Week 4

16. Be Aware of Microcultures

Compliance officers are always seeking innovative ways to instill a culture of compliance in their companies. New research suggests we need awareness of both the company's culture as a whole, and of microcultures that develop within departments, business units, regions, countries, and offices. When you're delivering messages or training, think about how these microcultures might respond. Then tweak your messaging accordingly to increase receptivity and acceptance in different microcultures.

17. Hire character, then train skill. — *Howard Schultz, longtime Starbucks CEO*

At some point in our careers, most of us will hire an assistant or junior compliance officer. While it's tempting to look for candidates with 100% of the necessary experience, try searching for both experience and intangible personal qualities. Skills can be learned and improved upon, but characteristics like stick-to-it-iveness and confidence can be hard to build. Hire bright people with good character, even if they don't have all the experience you'd like. You'll be glad you did.

18. Find Images Worth Investigating

Have you ever seen a presenter who offered no explanation for using a peculiar picture on a slide? If so, you probably began trying to decipher the picture's meaning. People love puzzles. An unexpected picture on a slide is an automatic hook. How can you make this work? Maybe you can share a for-eign-language road sign to explain "Stop!" A picture of a bridge could be used as a metaphor for where you've been and where you're going. Leveraging images creates intrigue and stokes curiosity, increasing engagement and helping others listen more closely to your presentation.

19. Take the Two Characteristics of Great Goals Test

Famed author Dr. Joe Vitale said that a good goal should scare you a little and excite you a lot. Being a little bit scared means your goal gets you out of your comfort zone, while exciting goals help you prioritize and keep your at-tention. See if your goals pass the exciting and scary test. If they do, congrat-ulations — you're on your way to success.

20. Dig in the Right Places

"If you're digging in the wrong place, stop digging." This cliché is correct. Evaluate your career. Are you in a dead-end job with no likelihood of promo-tion? Are you constantly assigned the same tasks with no opportunity for growth? If you're digging and digging and haven't hit gold, perhaps it is time to mine somewhere else. By evaluating your progress or lack thereof, you'll avoid weeks, months, or years of stagnation.

REFLECTION FRIDAY

Use the space below to record any thoughts, feelings, insights, or ideas that arose during the month. You might want to jot down anecdotes from personal relationships, examples from your workday, or anything that you want to internalize and take away from this month.

_____
_____
_____
_____

The Big Win

This week

_____
_____
_____
_____
_____
_____
_____

I'm Gonna Do It

The tip I've chosen to implement is number _____.
I'm going to implement it by

_____
_____
_____
_____
_____
_____
_____

Investigations

nvestigations can be one of the most interesting parts of the compliance officer's job. From illicit love affairs to stealing office supplies, investigations let our inner Sherlock Holmes take over to solve the mystery.

Compliance investigations can take various forms, but they may involve whistleblowers. When we're trying to protect someone who has found the courage to put themselves at risk to do what's right, the stakes are high. We feel personally invested in the outcome and want to help. Retaliation for doing the right thing is ugly to watch. Our job is to ensure that doesn't happen.

Sometimes, reports of misconduct are anonymous, making investigations frustratingly difficult to execute. We wish the person who sounded the alarm would reveal their identity. That way, we could get the necessary details to do our investigation properly.

And sometimes, investigations make us feel really bad. We watch an otherwise good employee who made a critical mistake get fired for out-of-character choices that leave us with an obligation to let them go.

Investigations also help us understand the root cause of misconduct. If we don't know why it happened, we can't adjust our programs to help ensure it doesn't happen again.

Investigative skills must be honed over time. Trust your gut, read the documents, perform the interviews, and write up the memos. Then do it again. There will never be a shortage of opportunities to grow.

Applying the Structure to You

The purpose of most investigations is to get to the bottom of what happened. That's no easy task. People have conflicting memories. He said one thing and she said another. Someone meant a comment in jest, but the listener took offense. Making final determinations can be tricky.

The job of a compliance officer is a hard and often lonely one. It is easy to feel that our work is being dismissed, or that we've been abandoned in our quest for an ethical culture. Even so, we must stay the course. Likewise, sometimes it takes digging deep and investigating our own feelings to get to the bottom of what's happening inside ourselves.

All of us have gone through periods where we feel depressed, uneasy, and restless. But sometimes, there's more going on beneath the surface. When you ask yourself why you're unhappy and the answer is "I don't know", an internal investigation should take place. And by internal, I mean within yourself.

Grief is painful. In the months after my father died, I found myself listless and uninterested in life. As time healed me, my feelings changed from depression to restlessness and discomfort. I couldn't pinpoint the source of my uneasiness. After all, I was the Chief Compliance Officer at United International Pictures (UIP), the joint distribution company of Paramount and Universal Pictures in London. It was a truly awesome job. I traveled the world to do training and attend movie premieres.

I loved working in entertainment after I graduated college. Going to work at UIP felt like coming home. So why was I so unhappy?

After a lot of soul-searching, I realized that the internal call to start my own company was getting louder. I looked inward to be sure I wasn't still responding to the grief and sadness associated with my dad's death. I wasn't.

At my core, I wanted to be an entrepreneur. I had wanted to make partner at the law firm I had worked at. I chose to stay in London and pursued compliance rather than go back to Los Angeles to continue in private practice.

But the dream of having multiple clients and running my own consulting projects never faded. My father was only 68 when he died. Death puts perspective on time. The platitude that "life is short" grew into full-fledged momentum for me to start my business.

As the publication date for How to Be a Wildly Effective Compliance Officer inched closer, I knew there would never be a better time to start my company. But I was terrified. What if I failed? What if we went broke or lost our house? What if I couldn't find another job easily if the company didn't make it? Once again, I did an internal investigation and decided that I was more afraid of never having tried than I was of failure. It was worth it.

January 31, 2016, was my last day at UIP. On February 1, 2016, I officially opened Spark Compliance. I've never looked back. I'm glad that I took the time to sort out grief, unease, restlessness, and discomfort to find what was truly causing me to feel ready to move to the next adventure.

What's causing your malaise?

What areas of your life are causing sadness or restlessness? Perhaps it's your romantic relationship (or lack of one). Perhaps a strained friendship is weighing on you. Perhaps you're feeling resentful of your job and angry that you must keep going when you don't want to. Take five minutes to write down everything that's been bugging you over the past month. You may want to use a separate piece of paper.

_____

_____

_____

_____

_____

_____

_____

Now, ask yourself what is really bothering you, then ask what you can do about it. Do you need to leave the situation? Do you need to find a new job or a new partner? Or would that not solve the problem because ultimately, what you need is to take better care of yourself? Do you need to change jobs?

Or start a business? Or do you actually need to stand up for yourself in your current job and set (and hold) boundaries? Write about it here:

_____

_____

_____

_____

_____

_____

_____

_____

Going Forward

During this period, get to the heart of your complicated emotions. When you're feeling sad or dissatisfied, perform an internal investigation. It may not be easy to suss out the root cause of our malaise, but it is worth sitting with the discomfort until you can figure it out. What we perceive as negative emotions can be the seat of wisdom. They tell us that we need to change to find our equilibrium. Listen to them.

WEEK 1

1. Controversial Decision? Document It

Compliance officers often have to fight the tough fight. When you lose a battle, make sure you document the outcome, preferably in an email. Let's say that you are making the case for why a third party should have its contract terminated for bribery allegations. If the business objects to the termination, write an email acknowledging their decision to go forward, despite the concerns raised by compliance. Documenting the decision will help you to clear your name if the incident is ever investigated, which can protect your career and reputation.

2. Explain Yourself

"Because" is a powerful word. People like to understand the reasoning behind your decisions and actions. When you offer explanations to others, use the word "because." A study in New York found that when people explain the reason for their request using the word "because," they were over 50% more likely to have their request granted. Use this to your advantage.

3. It's Okay Not to Know Everything

When you don't know the answer to a question, don't be afraid to say, "I'll find out and get right back to you." Many times, we feel like we're supposed to have all of the answers. We feel pressure to know everything or fake it when we don't. People respect someone who means it when they say, "I'm not sure, but I'll find out." You'll solve the problem and buy yourself time to think it over before you commit to an answer or a decision.

4. Speak First

Have you ever experienced that awkward moment in a meeting when the leader asks the group a question, only to be met with radio silence? If you know the answer or have something to share, speak up. Studies show that the first person to respond to the first question in a meeting is immediately considered a leader. This perception tends to last throughout the meeting and can influence how people see you going forward. Be brave, and speak first. Your reputation as a leader will follow.

5. What's in a Name? Everything!

Did you know that a person's name is typically their favorite word in the world? Remembering names is one of the best ways to demonstrate attention and engagement. One way to commit names to memory is to immediately associate them with a picture in your mind. For instance, if you meet someone named Austin, think of them standing on a map of the state of Texas. If you meet someone named May, picture them on a calendar for the fifth month.

Remembering names is a powerful way to show someone that you're genuinely glad to meet them.

The Big Win

This week

_____

_____

_____

_____

_____

_____

_____

I'm Gonna Do It

The tip I've chosen to implement is number _____.

I'm going to implement it by

_____

_____

_____

_____

_____

_____

_____

WEEK 2

6. Think Like a Criminal

We all like to believe that the controls we put in place will be effective — so much so that it often hinders our ability to look critically at our creations.

When you've come up with a new control, consider how you would get around it if you were a criminal. Work to find a nefarious way to circumvent the control. If you can't work your way around the control, congratulations — it should stay in place. By adopting the mindset of a criminal, you'll gain a deeper understanding of the control's real-world effectiveness, and be able to improve upon it.

7. Adopt a Confidence Mindset

When you're feeling unsure or find yourself in an unfamiliar environment, try acting with confidence even if you don't feel it. Many of us get flustered or frightened when doing in-person training in an unfamiliar country or presenting at our first board meeting. By acting as though we're confident and taking on the stance of a powerful person, we give ourselves the opportunity to mimic those who believe in themselves, which in turn boosts confidence — for real. Act the part long enough, and you're likely to naturally become more powerful and poised.

8. Don't Let Emotions Overcome You

If you become embroiled in a heated conversation or you find yourself on the verge of an argument, take a beat to recenter before you respond. Strategies like imagining yourself outside of your body and watching the interaction from a distance can help you settle. If you can pull yourself back from an impulsive emotional response and return to your logical self, you're better poised to thwart a confrontation and refocus the conversation, bringing you back to a place where progress is possible.

9. Avoid Catastrophizing

Have you ever heard a snippet of negative information, then immediately assumed the worst-case scenario? We all have, but when we don't know the backstory, we can choose to put a positive spin on the information instead of spiraling to a dark place. Let's say your boss barked at you on the phone this morning. You can choose to believe that you're going to get fired, or you can tell yourself that she's having a bad day because her boss just yelled at her. When you don't know the whole story, shift your mindset and avoid catastrophizing.

10. Check Your Bias

When you're performing an internal investigation, stay neutral until all the facts are in. It's human nature to develop a point of view and then look for facts or information that confirm it. But in an internal investigation, neutrality is critical. By recognizing that your instinct is to not be neutral, you can work to ensure a fair outcome for all parties involved.

The Big Win

This week

_____

_____

_____

_____

_____

_____

_____

I'm Gonna Do It

The tip I've chosen to implement is number _____.

I'm going to implement it by

_____

_____

_____

_____

_____

_____

WEEK 3

11. Turn the Clock Back for Meetings

Scheduling a meeting with people in multiple time zones can get messy. An easy way to see when you're available is to momentarily change the clock setting on your computer to the other time zones. When you open your calendar, you'll see your existing meetings in the new time zone. That way, whether you're offering or confirming your availability, you'll be certain you're right on time.

12. Be Patient in the Beginning

A change in management or leadership at a company often comes with a big shift in how employees relate to compliance. In many industries, compliance hasn't fully developed as a career, and new leaders may not understand the impact of your work. Building relationships with the new leaders is important, and may require educating them about your role and its direct value to the organization. If this takes some time, have patience. New leaders can become great advocates, but first, they need to understand the importance of compliance.

13. What's the Question?

Is there a way to start a training or presentation that's guaranteed to engage your audience? Simple: try starting with a question. Whether the question is rhetorical or solicits an answer, you'll immediately get listeners engaged in answering your question. This will kick off the presentation or training on the right foot, and communicate to your audience that you are interested in their thoughts and experience.

14. Elevate Your Training with Facts and Stories

When we're feeling nervous before a presentation, resist the temptation to rush through the main points. Instead of barreling through your slides, go steady and remember to add in stories and facts or quotes. Stories engage the right side of the brain, which regulates emotions. Facts or quotes typically engage the left side of the brain, which responds to logic and reason. When you engage both sides of the brain, your presentation will be more memorable and engaging, and therefore, more effective.

15. Assume the Best

You're probably familiar with the sinking feeling that comes when we receive a message from an adversary. But pause before assuming the worst. A negative mindset makes us more inclined to read negative undertones that a neutral person would never sense in the same text. When you receive a message from a challenging person, take a beat before listening to the voicemail or reading the email. Choose to believe that they're genuinely trying their best. Ignore any rogue statements, then get straight down to business. You'll temper your stress, which will make your response more effective.

The Big Win

This week

_____

_____

_____

_____

_____

_____

_____

I'm Gonna Do It

The tip I've chosen to implement is number _____.

I'm going to implement it by

_____

_____

_____

_____

_____

_____

_____

WEEK 4

16. Think Like a Physician

Sometimes, despite your best efforts, you can't convince the business to invest in an aspect of your program. Perhaps you need a travel budget to perform in-person training or to do enhanced due diligence on your highest-risk third parties. When you've tried every avenue but still can't find a way to yes, imagine that you're a physician. A doctor can tell a patient to stop smoking or lose weight, but ultimately, it's the patient's decision. The same goes for businesses: you can't force them to act in their own interest. Offer your best advice, advocate for your position, and then let it go.

17. Get Intel from Your Auditors

Internal Auditors typically spend much more time in remote locations than you do, so build a good relationship with them. Try to have a short call with the lead auditor whenever they come and go from a new location. You'll keep compliance concerns top of mind while doing recognizance about the feel of the location. Internal Audit is unlikely to write details in a report like, "They seem really overworked and the sales goals are impossibly high. I'm not sure we're incentivizing them properly," but they might tell you that on a phone call. Consistent conversations with auditors can provide key intel about the scene on the ground.

18. Keep Honesty Civil

We all know that honesty and transparency are critical parts of our function. However, there are times when blunt honesty veers into rudeness. Pay attention to your tone and choice of words when you're delivering difficult news. Be especially vigilant of your tone when you're giving a review. Honesty may be required but rudeness is never acceptable, even when you're speaking the truth.

19. Yes, You Need an Introduction

Did you know that being introduced before you speak immediately identifies you as a leader? If you're scheduled to make a presentation, be sure to ask someone to introduce you. Even a quick intro with your name and role adds formality and importance to your speech or training session. If no one has offered, simply ask someone who will be at the meeting to present you. An introduction will make your messages more respected and remembered.

20. The Riches Are in the Niches

In entrepreneurship, they say the riches are in the niches. Many successful businesses find a specialized market segment and flourish. To apply this to your career, find something you like and become a true expert in it. Perhaps you can be the go-to expert for data privacy at your company or the master of trade sanctions screening. For greater success, pick your niche and dive deep.

REFLECTION FRIDAY

Use the space below to record any thoughts, feelings, insights, or ideas that arose during the month. You might want to jot down anecdotes from personal relationships, examples from your workday, or anything that you want to internalize and take away from this month.

_____

_____

_____

_____

The Big Win

This week

_____

_____

_____

_____

_____

_____

_____

I'm Gonna Do It

The tip I've chosen to implement is number _____.

I'm going to implement it by

_____

_____

_____

_____

_____

_____

_____

Incentives

Incentives shouldn't be a taboo topic in compliance, and yet, so often they are. Senior leaders often bristle at the idea that they should reward employees for compliant behavior or acting ethically. "Why should we incentivize people to do their job?" they say while creating a commission structure that incentivizes salespeople to make sales (which is, by the way, the salesperson's job).

Incentives drive behavior. When faced with two equally important tasks, humans will choose the one that provides the greater reward. We know this instinctively. Reward systems are developed to inspire the desired behavior.

Incentives can reward qualitative behavior, quantitative behavior, or both. Quantitative behavior can be measured. For instance, "Did you take your compliance training by the deadline?" is a quantitative yes/no question. You either did or you didn't.

Qualitative behavior can be tougher. "Did you model ethical decision-making?" is inherently subjective. But it can still be an important consideration for promotions and bonuses.

In business, incentives tell employees about the company's priorities. If compliance is limited to using discipline to reinforce behavior and cannot offer incentives, there is an imbalance. Ideally, compliance officers should have the ability to use incentives to inspire people to do the right thing and discipline them when necessary.

Applying the Structure to You

Humans can be so critical of themselves. How often have you said things to yourself that you would be horrified to hear someone say to another person? Most of us are great at self-punishment but not good at incentivizing the behavior we want from ourselves.

Many teachers set up incentive systems in their classrooms. Kids can earn stickers or candy bars for doing well on quizzes or completing homework on time. Likewise, smart parents put together reward systems to incentivize desired behaviors. Mine did.

When I was about seven, a local amusement park called Knott's Berry Farm opened a new roller coaster. The advertisements were everywhere, and I was entranced. I've always been a thrill seeker. Even at the age of seven, I knew that speed was my friend.

I asked my mom to take me to the park. She declined. I asked again. Again, no. Then I tried whining. That was deeply unsuccessful. I would not let it go. I asked every day. Finally, Mom set out a list of chores that I could do for three months to earn the ability to go to Knott's Berry Farm. The list included making my bed every day, keeping my room clean, helping her garden, making breakfast for my sisters, clearing the table after dinner, and going to bed on time without fuss. I got a gold star on the poster every day I succeeded.

Did I make it? You better believe it. I happily completed each task. Every day I thought about how much fun I was going to have at the park, and when the day came to go upside down on a track made of steel, I was 100% ready.

I went on that roller coaster and every other one in the park over and over again until my Mom dragged me out.

I still love roller coasters. These days, I might incentivize myself with trips to the amusement park, but also with trips ten minutes from my house to walk on the beach when I finish my work. I incentivize myself by going out to dinner, playing games, soaking in our hot tub, buying fresh flowers, taking a dance class, going to concerts, getting a massage, listening to a non-work-related podcast, taking a drive on a winding road with the top down on the car, having a nice bottle of wine, or watching romantic reality TV (oh how I love The Bachelor — no judging). Sometimes the simple things make the best incentives.

When I'm having a hard day at work or am feeling uninspired, I'll choose a reward to inspire me to finish my tasks. It helps.

How do you incentivize yourself?

What motivates you? Many of us were taught to believe that harsh discipline was the best way to correct our "bad" behavior. That's why it's common to self-flagellate when we make mistakes or fail to meet the high standards we set for ourselves. But self-care is a better motivator than shame.

What can you use to replace self-beratement with personal happiness? How can aligned incentives help you boost satisfaction? Name 20 things you enjoy. Why 20? Because we want to have a great variety to choose from. Pick free things (taking a relaxing walk, watching cat videos on YouTube) and more expensive options. Pick active and passive options. Choose rich lingering indulgences and quick-shot, feel-good alternatives.

1. _____
2. _____
3. _____
4. _____
5. _____
6. _____
7. _____
8. _____
9. _____
10. _____
11. _____
12. _____
13. _____
14. _____
15. _____
16. _____
17. _____
18. _____

19. _____

20. _____

Keep this list handy whenever you're feeling unmotivated to do the things you need to do. Whether it's inspiring yourself to go to that networking event or making yourself take that class at the gym, have an incentive to drive your success.

Going Forward

Use this period to identify things that bring you joy. Take those experiences and add them to your list. Find ways to pair difficult or dull activities with an incentive to complete them. Swap out self-punishment and negative self-talk for incentives and celebration of success. Be conscious of how you're structuring your wins and what you do in response. Most of all, incentivize the behavior you want from yourself. That way, you'll get more of it!

WEEK 1

1. Say No When You Mean No

Have you ever said yes to a social or charitable request that you wished you'd politely declined? Instead of kicking yourself for going against your better judgment, decline quickly and decisively if the request isn't work-critical. Say something like, "Unfortunately I won't be able to make it, but I'm sure it'll be a terrific event." For charitable activities, consider, "Unfortunately, our charitable giving budget is already set for the year." Letting someone down is uncomfortable at the moment, but it's easier than managing obligations or the sense of dread when you ultimately bow out.

2. Book Flights Faster

If you travel frequently, you know a few minutes can make a big difference, so be sure to create a list of all of your frequent flier numbers and other loyalty program numbers in Word or Outlook. Frequent travelers may be enrolled in many programs, and searching for your numbers whenever you book a flight creates unnecessary work for you and the people who make your life easier. If you have administrative help or a travel agent, share your list so everyone has easy access to your numbers. It will make you one happy traveler.

3. Speaking of Speaker Recommendations

If you've got a good title, chances are you're on every conference producer's list. While it's great to be asked, speaking at conferences can take a lot of time, not to mention travel. If you're turning down an opportunity, give the conference producer alternative options. Identify someone in your department who would love the opportunity, or find someone in your local community. You can help the producer, your colleagues, and your community while expanding the list of people known as good speakers.

4. Get on the Same Side — Literally

If you're requesting resources, having a difficult conversation, or engaging in a tough negotiation, pay attention to your positioning and try not to sit directly across from the other party. Sitting across from someone can be perceived as adversarial, whereas sitting next to the other party or at an angle to them will psychologically show that you're "on the same side."

5. Put Compliance @ Your Fingertips

Consider requesting the email address Compliance@[yourcompany].com. People in the business often can't remember the name of their compliance lead, or they may have trouble spelling it. With a generic compliance@ email address, you create a simple, memorable address for people to direct their compliance concerns. In addition, if someone leaves the business, the Compliance@ email address remains, eliminating the need to reprint posters or other communication tools with a name on them.

The Big Win

This week

_____

_____

_____

_____

_____

_____

_____

I'm Gonna Do It

The tip I've chosen to implement is number _____.

I'm going to implement it by

_____

_____

_____

_____

_____

_____

_____

WEEK 2

6. Choose a Good Board

Your company has a Board of Directors, and so should you. Choose people for your board that you admire, including those you don't know personally. When you have a tough decision to make, consult your board in your mind. Perhaps your board includes Gandhi, Oprah, and the President of the United States. Great! What do they think? Hearing their advice in your head can lead to surprisingly useful insights.

7. A Great Way to Create Greater Engagement

Do you want to increase engagement with your initiatives? We all do. A surefire way to do so is to get others involved with crafting initiatives. Consider asking business leaders to participate in a brief roundtable to create communications that will be well received by their teams. Or ask ten middle managers to tell you about the ethical dilemmas they've faced so you can model training scenarios using their experiences. The more people are directly involved with an initiative, the more they're likely to promote it. After all, the ideas came from them, so they must be good.

8. Transpose Percentages for High Impact

Have you ever seen eyes glaze over when telling stories of sky-high compliance-related fines? Because "four billion dollars" isn't a number most executives can comprehend (much less apply to their business), people may tune out. If huge numbers aren't registering, try calculating the percentage of revenue that the fine represents, and then apply it to your company. For instance, let's say the $4 billion bribery fine had been applied to a company with $70 billion in revenue. That's about 6%. If your company makes $15 million in revenue, the equivalent fine would be $900,000. That number will likely have a stronger emotional effect on your senior executives; they can imagine its impact on the company. By making exorbitant fines real to your executives, you're likely to get the buy-in you need to avoid them in the first place.

9. Be Ignorant of Procedures

Subject matter experts frequently find it difficult to write good procedures because they assume the reader has more knowledge than they do. When you've written a procedure, challenge yourself to only follow the directions you've written. By acting as if you're totally ignorant, you can see whether your procedure effectively moves the reader from start to finish.

10. Tough Situation? Find You Advantage

Let's face it, sometimes really bad things happen to us at work. You might get passed over for a promotion, or have a big-budget item denied. You might even get fired or made redundant. No matter what challenge presents itself, ask yourself, "How does this work to my advantage?" Your first answer will likely be, "It doesn't!" But keep asking yourself the question. Maybe not getting that promotion means you'll learn new skills in your current role. Maybe you'll find a workaround to your limited budget that shows your creativity within constraints. Maybe being let go is the first step toward another, more exciting opportunity. You never know what lies just up ahead.

The Big Win

This week

_____
_____
_____
_____
_____
_____
_____

I'm Gonna Do It

The tip I've chosen to implement is number _____.
I'm going to implement it by

_____
_____
_____
_____
_____
_____
_____

11. Not Getting Anywhere? Initiate a Walk and Talk

We've all been there. You're having a disagreement, and you can't seem to get anywhere with the other party despite intense negotiations. Instead of getting angry, try scheduling a walking meeting so you can discuss the issue outside the office. You'll naturally stand side-by-side in a non-confrontational position. By literally going in the same direction, you're more likely to find a fresh point of view, and in turn land on a compromise that satisfies you both.

12. You Feel Fantastic

It's likely your coworkers ask the same question every day: "How's your day?" or "How are you doing?" "Busy" or "stressful" are common replies, but did you know that a positive response can actually make your day better? Try "Fantastic," "Great" or "It's going really well." It's hard not to smile when you respond, and you just might elicit a smile from others, too.

13. Be a Connector

As you're building your network, take time to introduce people who share common interests and experiences. For instance, if someone in your network is moving from New York to Boston, send email introductions to your contacts in Boston. Not sure who is in Boston? Use LinkedIn to find out. The more you foster connections within your network, the stronger your network will be.

14. Initiate a Gathering

To combat compliance officers' bad reputation as killjoys, organize a social event at least once a year. It can be as simple as a birthday lunch or a happy hour, or as elaborate as an outdoor summer soiree. Invite people you're close with and those you'd like to get to know better. By organizing the event, you'll be the hub of social activity, making it easier for others to approach you and get to know you better.

15. Sweeten the Deal

What's everyone's favorite place to go for a mid-afternoon pick-me-up? The candy jar, of course! Make your desk the most popular place on the floor by keeping a well-stocked candy jar. You'll draw people in, and they'll naturally get to know you. By simply filling a candy jar, your desk will become the go-to for sweets and conversation.

The Big Win

This week

_____
_____
_____
_____
_____
_____
_____

I'm Gonna Do It

The tip I've chosen to implement is number _____.
I'm going to implement it by

_____
_____
_____
_____
_____
_____
_____

WEEK 4

16. Pay Attention to the Pace of Speech

You may know the value of mirroring body language, but did you know that mirroring the speed and tone of your conversation partner is also important? Note whether the person you're chatting with speaks faster or slower than your natural speed. Speaking slowly when someone is speaking quickly may make them feel like you're lethargic or preventing them from getting work done. Speaking quickly to someone speaking slowly may make them feel anxious or like you're rushing to get off the phone. Adjusting your speech can make your conversation partner feel more comfortable. In other words, you'll be "exactly their speed."

17. Make a (Visual) Impression

Countless presentations use boring graphs and bar charts. It's a snooze, so think carefully about ways to spice up the statistics in your next presentation. Can you change up the visuals to show numbers as the height of different mountains? How about comparing the relative sizes of candies — say M&Ms versus bubble gum balls — to illustrate differences? At the very least, add animations so your graph has movement and visual interest. The more unexpected visuals you include, the more you'll capture your audience's attention.

18. Ask in the Affirmative

Asking for time off for personal reasons can be tricky. How can you stack the deck in your favor? If you're emailing a request, assume the answer is yes. "I'm going to take Tuesday off for a personal appointment," or "I'm going to go with option number two" are great ways to start. Finish the request with, "if I don't hear otherwise from you," or "please let me know if this is not acceptable to you." This way, you put the ball in the respondent's court. If they don't respond with an objection, then assume you've obtained permission.

19. Prioritize Deep Work

Taking time for deep work is critical. To perform at your best, you need uninterrupted time to focus on big tasks – especially creative tasks or those requiring extensive drafting. If you're worried that people will need you, let them know that they can call you any time if it's urgent. You're likely not to get any calls, and your productivity will soar.

20. Boldly Highlight Action Items

The average worker gets 121 emails per day. With all that noise, it's easy for others to miss the actions you need to complete, especially when the email is to more than one person. Bold or highlight a person's name when asking a direct question or assigning an action item. The person is infinitely more likely to respond if their name is made obvious.

REFLECTION FRIDAY

Use the space below to record any thoughts, feelings, insights, or ideas that arose during the month. You might want to jot down anecdotes from personal relationships, examples from your workday, or anything that you want to internalize and take away from this month.

_____
_____
_____
_____

The Big Win

This week

_____
_____
_____
_____
_____

_____

_____

_____

I'm Gonna Do It

The tip I've chosen to implement is number _____.

I'm going to implement it by

_____

_____

_____

_____

_____

_____

_____

Your Quarterly Audit

t's time to reflect on the four tips you chose to implement. This evaluation is important because the repetitive acknowledgment of your goals and actions keeps you on track.

Part 1: EVALUATION

Directions: Write the number of each tip you implemented, and check each box that applies. Some tips might apply across the board, while others only relate to one category.

Tip. No.	Completed Tip	Lead to greater work success	Improved my non-work life	Both

Part 2: REFLECTION

1. Which tips will you carry through to the next quarter?

_____

_____

_____

2. Which tips influence your mental space? (positive thinking, achievement, and goal setting)

_____

_____

_____

3. Which tips changed your physical space? (Your home office, at-work desk, etc.)

_____

_____

_____

4. Which tips came naturally to you, and which forced you to step out of your comfort zone?

_____

_____

_____

5. Which is/are part of a larger push toward improvement in one area of your life?

_____

_____

_____

6.   Which revealed existing strengths, and which showed areas of improvement? Weaknesses?

_____

_____

_____

7.   *Bonus*: Which one are you going to share with others?

_____

_____

_____

Monitoring and Metrics

You're three-quarters of the way through your year as a Wildly Effective Compliance Officer. Pat yourself on the back and congratulate yourself for sticking with it! You've now written down months of wins to fuel your performance review and to remind yourself of how good you are at your job.

You've also identified useful tips and tricks to increase productivity, strengthen relationships, deepen connections with your colleagues, expand your network, and influence the business more successfully.

This is the last quarter of the year, and we want to end it with a bang. In Q4, we will focus on the themes of monitoring and metrics, reporting, and continuous improvement.

Monitoring and Metrics

We need to know if our program is succeeding, and that's where monitoring comes in. Monitoring simply means paying attention and tracking what is working and what is not.

The most well-intentioned initiatives sometimes fail. It's important to know early if an initiative isn't performing as expected so you can pivot. Monitoring can also help you identify trends and spot problems early.

Metrics are defined as a method of measuring something, or the results obtained when measuring. Metrics allow us to analyze our monitoring activity so we can draw informed conclusions.

The DOJ and other regulators are focusing more and more on our ability to measure the effectiveness of our programs and their sub-parts. The DOJ, in its Evaluation of Corporate Compliance Programs guidance, asks us how we are evaluating the effectiveness of our training and our risk management. Metrics enable us to do that.

Good data is critical to effective monitoring and metrics analysis. More programs are utilizing data analytics and hiring data scientists to create a more sophisticated monitoring program. We are likely to see that trend continue over time.

Applying the Structure to You

Just as it is important to monitor the success of your program, it is also important to monitor the success of the initiatives in your own life. Whether it is strengthening your body, debt decrease or wealth increase, or learning a new skill, monitoring helps you to stay on track — or to identify where you veered off course. Metrics will help you to quantify what is working.

The most difficult parts of monitoring and metrics tend to be identifying what to track, and how to consistently obtain the information necessary to do so.

Lawyers often joke that they became lawyers because they weren't good at math. I identified with that, which created major challenges in the early years of Spark Compliance. It's not that I didn't track the number of contracts signed and cash flowing in and out. It's that I had no consistent way of monitoring what was happening.

This lack of monitoring led to a cash flow crisis at times. Bills needed to be paid, as did employees' health insurance premiums. I never knew with certainty how much I could pay myself, which resulted in overpayments (and later cash challenges) or underpayment, leaving me vulnerable to an unexpected bill.

I knew enough to create an annual estimated budget, but it wasn't a living document that guided the company well throughout the year. We were doing the proverbial flying the plane while building it — and frequently, just winging it.

At our wits' end, the Spark Compliance owners hired a business coach who insisted that we create a 12-week rolling cash flow Excel sheet. The 12-week, as it is affectionately called, identifies every expense the business is expecting as well as all its expected income.

At first, we resisted the 12-week. For me, it felt like a pedantic waste of time that was better spent writing, speaking, selling, or working on client projects. For Jonathan, it was uncomfortable to guess what revenue and expenses looked like three months out when it wasn't concrete. Guessing felt unsafe.

Every client has slightly different terms, and the 12-week helped us to identify exactly when we should expect money to come in. Spark's employees work varying numbers of billable hours each month. The 12-week helps us forecast a bump or lull in the payroll. It also helps us to plan for big expenses like conference exhibitions and travel for the Sparkies.

Jonathan and I have committed to updating and going over the 12-week every Wednesday. To say it's changed the business for the better is a massive understatement. It turns out that I really do like math when it's working in favor of making my business stronger and more resilient.

The information I've gotten from the 12-week has made me an infinitely better CEO. I'm better prepared and can make more informed decisions. Monitoring our cash flow with the 12-week tool is critical to my progress. It's one of the most important things I've ever done in my professional life.

What are you tracking?

Choose one or more of the initiatives you've started or want to start. If you've chosen a professional goal like receiving a certification, you can monitor your progress toward your goal. If you're learning a new skill like a language, you can monitor your pace at completing the classes or modules.

What initiative are you going to review?

_____

_____

_____

_____

Think of as many ways as you can to potentially monitor your progress.

_____

_____

_____

_____

Pick one way to monitor your progress. Write it here.

_____

_____

_____

_____

Now think about the metric you can use to judge your success. Is there a number you can track to show the speed of your progress toward your goal? If you achieve your goal, is there a metric that can show consistency in its achievement or tell you if you're getting off track? Write your ideas for metrics here:

_____

_____

_____

_____

Going Forward

Use this period to consider ways to monitor what matters to you. If you've committed to becoming more physically active, monitor how often you go to the gym or for a walk. Track the weekly number and use it as a metric to determine whether you're meeting your goal.

If you've committed to expanding your network, monitor how frequently you go on LinkedIn and comment or post. Use the number as a metric to determine whether you're achieving what you set out to do.

Data brings clarity, and clarity can change behavior to help you reach your goals.

WEEK 1

1. Make Compliance Convenient

People are busy, and anything that hinders their workflow creates a problem. When you need employees to complete important tasks like training or entering expenses into the gifts and hospitality tracker, make the process as frictionless as possible. For training or due diligence platforms, get a single sign-on so that employees don't need multiple usernames or passwords. For the gifts and hospitality tracker, use drop-down menus so employees don't have to type excessively. The easier and more convenient you make it to comply, the more people will do so.

2. Save Time with Automated Emails

There's an easy way to automate emails you write over and over again using the "Signature" function in Outlook. For example, draft a new signature and title it, "Respond to due diligence request." When you get an email about due diligence requests, respond by adding in the due diligence signature. This will give you the template to work from, making your response time lightning fast.

3. Travel a New Path

Most of us walk the same way through the office every day. Whether it's a walk to the car, the break room, or the restroom, we tend to operate on autopilot. Instead of taking the same path, consciously switch up your routine for a week. Walk a different way to your car. Go to a break room on a different floor to get a coffee. Walk to someone's office to say hello instead of sending an email. By altering your routine, you'll change who you see and interact with. Your internal network will grow, reminding people that compliance is there to help.

4. Working from Home? Stick to Your Schedule

One drawback of remote work is that you can work at any time...which can easily snowball into working all the time. Instead of starting and stopping work whenever you feel like it, set work hours as you would in an office. Knowing when you start and stop can help set expectations for your co-workers and make you seem more reliable because you'll be present and available on a consistent schedule. Even better, you can plan your evenings or mornings. You'll get more joy from your time outside of work if you set boundaries and don't feel like you should be at your computer all the time.

5. Cancel Meetings Without an Agenda

So much time is wasted in meetings and on phone calls that lack a clear objective. If your meeting doesn't have an agenda, cancel or reschedule it for a time when you'll have clarity about the plan. Don't request meetings or phone calls if you don't have an agenda. Don't demure when people who request calls or meetings can't provide you with an agenda. By sifting out meetings that are likely to be unproductive, you'll free your time up for more useful and important work.

The Big Win

This week

_____
_____
_____
_____
_____
_____
_____

I'm Gonna Do It

The tip I've chosen to implement is number _____.

I'm going to implement it by

_____
_____
_____
_____
_____
_____
_____

WEEK 2

6. Inform People When Priorities Change

Whenever disaster strikes, it's easy to get completely caught up in what needs to be done next. A data breach, regulatory investigation, or critical third-party that suddenly appears on the sanctions list can wreak havoc on the business. When this happens, it's vitally important that you tell those who count on you for responses or your usual work that you're unable to deliver on time because of the issue. If the fire is confidential, simply say that you're unable to deliver on time. Give them a timeframe for when you'll be back to normal operating hours. By preemptively telling them you've got other priorities, you'll ensure that they don't have lingering resentment or mistrust going forward.

7. Set Up Google Alerts

As a busy professional, it can be hard to stay on top of all the pending changes that affect your industry or how you do your job. Thankfully, there's Google Alerts, which sends emails to your inbox on a regular basis alerting you to news about topics of your choice. Let's say you work in the fishing industry, and a new law could potentially affect your company's supply chain. By creating a Google Alert, you can stay on top of its developments via notifications. Then, when the law comes into force, you'll have a long runway to implement programmatic changes in order to comply.

8. Flag it for Follow-Up

Declutter your inbox by red-flagging emails that you need to respond to but can't do so immediately. When you click the flag in Outlook, the email will turn red, making it easy to see. You can separate these emails and then respond to them all at once, which makes it less likely that important emails will get lost or go unreturned.

9. Get Certified for Success

If we know we're great at our jobs, certificates can seem unimportant. But certifications prove your knowledge to the outside world. They can lead to job openings, promotions, and a bigger network. If you're able to get a certification, do it. The time and hassle are worth the effort for the opportunities certifications create.

10. Consider the True Cost of DIY

For many compliance officers with tight budgets, getting external help from consultants or technology solutions seems impossible. One way to justify the costs of outside help is to determine how long a project will take in-house, then compare that to outsourcing. Let's say you've been tasked with a risk assessment that will take an estimated 100 hours. Assuming you have other tasks and priorities, it could take three months. But if you have a professional consultant come in, the risk assessment could be completed in a month or less, giving you more time to implement the recommendations and controls. Giving the project over to a dedicated outside source means your time is freed up to complete the implementation and get the risk under control more quickly.

The Big Win

This week

_____

_____

_____

_____

_____

_____

_____

I'm Gonna Do It

The tip I've chosen to implement is number _____.

I'm going to implement it by

_____

_____

_____

_____

_____

_____

_____

Week 3:

11. Want People to Leave You Alone? Give Them a Sign

All of us know the frustration of getting interrupted when we're trying to get some writing or analyzing done. To train the people around you to know when you're busy thinking, come up with a sign. It may be a literal sign asking others not to interrupt you for an hour, to be placed on your desk or the side of your computer if you're in an open area. You can also put on headphones — the larger the better — so people get the hint that they shouldn't interrupt you. The more visible your sign, the better. You'll get your work done, and others will let you do it.

12. Price Isn't Only About Money

We tend to think of price in terms of dollars, pounds, or euros. But there are other currencies, like time and energy. When you're deciding whether an activity is worth it, think about the cost in every respect. It's one thing if a commitment costs a lot of money, but quite another if it costs money, time, and energy. The takeaway? Before committing to an activity, a piece of software, or an event, consider the cost in every sense of the word.

13. Outline to Optimize Your Writing

When you are writing reports or other long documents, be sure to outline your thoughts and the structure of the document on paper before you start writing. By writing down your ideas, you'll be able to form the structure of the document, ensuring you don't forget any important points. Writing from a structure makes it easier to complete the project, and will keep you from going off on tangents or writing too much in one section and not enough in another. It's worth the time to plan, as your writing will improve tremendously.

14. Doing it More Than Twice? Don't

Do you ever find yourself with a project or task you could hand off, but then you think, "Forget it, it'll be faster if I do it myself." Instead, stop and ask yourself this question: "Is this a task I'll need to do more than twice?" If it is a recurring task, take the time to write out instructions or walk another person through it. By taking the time to teach someone to do the work you can pass on, you'll save yourself time later, while giving the person you delegate to an opportunity to learn.

15. Know Your Destination

We all have 24 hours in the day, but our working hours can easily be consumed by low-value tasks and a constant string of menial to-dos. Instead of immediately tackling whatever hits your inbox, ask yourself this critical question: "Is this activity going to get me where I want to go?" If you know where you want to go — say, to a higher level in the company — then this question will clarify whether or not a certain activity will get you there, and help you come up with a metric to track progress. Focus on high-value tasks, and you'll get where you're going significantly sooner.

The Big Win

This week

_____

_____

_____

_____

_____

_____

_____

I'm Gonna Do It

The tip I've chosen to implement is number _____.
I'm going to implement it by

_____

_____

_____

_____

_____

_____

_____

Week 4

16. Take Ten Minutes to Plan Success

When you show up for work in the morning, do you find yourself overwhelmed with the tasks of the day? Instead of simply starting as soon as you sit down at your desk, take ten minutes to plan the major parts of your day. Look at your calendar, make a list of the most important activities, and note which project you will begin first. Then execute your plan. You'll get more done, be prepared to complete high-value tasks, and avoid wasting time.

17. Remove the Address for Complicated Emails

If you're writing a complicated email with detailed instructions, draft it first without any email addresses in the subject line. Add names in the address bar only after the email is edited and ready to go. Many emails seem to send themselves before you're ready, causing us stress or embarrassment. Add the addresses at the end and that problem is solved.

18. Calculate the Real Technology Cost

How much does technology cost or save? Much more than most people think. Employees, including those in compliance, frequently "zero rate" their time. Zero rating occurs when people don't consider the hourly cost of their employment. Let's say you want a third-party due diligence platform that will automatically screen third parties and perform continuous monitoring. If your hourly rate equates to $100 and it takes you three hours to process each third-party manually, your time will quickly add up to more than the cost of the platform. When asking for resources, be sure to calculate the cost of your time. You'll get to yes faster.

19. Repeat Names Immediately

Many people struggle to remember the names of people they've just met, but it doesn't have to be this way. When you meet someone, immediately say their name back to them to be sure you're pronouncing it correctly. Use it at least two more times in your initial conversation so that it sticks. Then, write it down when you're on your own, along with a detail or two about the individual. You'll be much more likely to remember the name, and that will make the person feel important when you next meet up.

20: Forward When You're Feeling Snarky

We've all cringed when someone accidentally hits "reply all" with a joke or snide remark to a group email when the reply was clearly meant only for one person. Instead of worrying whether you hit "reply" or "reply all," try "forward" instead. Forwarding requires proactively adding the recipient's names, which can save you embarrassment.

REFLECTION FRIDAY

Use the space below to record any thoughts, feelings, insights, or ideas that arose during the month. You might want to jot down anecdotes from personal relationships, examples from your workday, or anything that you want to internalize and take away from this month.

_____

_____

_____

_____

The Big Win

This week

_____

_____

_____

_____

_____

_____

_____

I'm Gonna Do It

The tip I've chosen to implement is number ____.

I'm going to implement it by

_____

_____

_____

_____

_____

_____

_____

Reporting

I n the last period, we covered monitoring and metrics. Monitoring activity and metrics typically flow up in an abbreviated format to the C-suite and board of directors. The board and senior leadership have a fiduciary duty to the company. If they are not properly attuned to compliance-related risks and overseeing the effectiveness of the program, in some cases they can be held personally liable for their failures. In other words, reporting matters.

Reporting is a very important skill. The best compliance officers use data to tell the story of how their program is succeeding, and where it needs support and better resources to be effective. There is an art to explaining risk, both upcoming and current, to the leadership team in a way that is frightening but not too frightening.

That's why it is critical to know your audience. You'll increase attention and engagement if you're telling them the information they want and need to know. Reporting on successes (e.g., after training, 98% of people passed the knowledge-based quiz) versus reporting on activities (e.g., we trained 100 people last quarter) is always a better bet. Know your audience, and understand what's important to them.

Reporting will hold you accountable for reaching your program goals. Each year, senior leaders like Chief Compliance Officers commit to milestones and goals for the program. Reporting keeps the CCO accountable and responsible for their commitments as well.

Applying the Structure to You

A great way to increase your likelihood of reaching a goal is to tell it to other people. Whether one-on-one or on social media, proclaiming your intention creates social pressure to reach the finish line.

To raise the stakes (and chances of success) even higher, ask a friend or their online community to hold them accountable for reaching their goal and encourage them to keep going when it gets tough.

Case in point: About two months into training for the marathon, I posted my goal on social media. Although I was only able to walk about seven miles at that point, I knew that by making my intentions public, I would be more committed to succeeding. Throughout the training process, I felt compelled to report my progress and share that I'd achieved my goal several months later.

In his book Think and Grow Rich, author Napoleon Hill suggests getting a group of like-minded individuals together to create mastermind groups. A mastermind group meets on a regular basis to talk to each other about business problems/opportunities, give each other feedback, and hold one another accountable for the actions they commit to taking.

I met Kirsten Liston of Rethink Compliance in the first six months I owned Spark Compliance. As described further in The Compliance Entrepreneur's Handbook (co-authored by myself, Kirsten, and Joe Murphy), Kirsten and I formed a two-person mastermind group to help each other run our businesses and succeed in the compliance industry.

We met every two weeks. The meetings were highly structured. We started by sharing our wins, then one of us would be in the "hot seat." The person in the hot seat brought an issue or problem they wanted to discuss. The other person listened, encouraged conversation, and supplied ideas. The meeting ended with each of us committing to actions before the next meeting. When the next meeting started, we'd go through "accountability", as we called it. We'd report back to each other on our progress.

As a mastermind meeting approached, I'd check back to make sure I'd fulfilled my commitments. Frequently, I ended up scrambling to complete them so I could report back to Kirsten that I had succeeded. This was highly benefi-cial because it kept me on track. Reporting to someone else made it real.

Ultimately, our offerings began to overlap, so Kirsten and I stopped our mastermind meetings. I still miss them sometimes. They were extremely help-ful, and the camaraderie was brilliant.

Who will you report to?

You don't have to create a formal mastermind group to obtain the bene-fits of reporting. Indeed, you can simply choose one or more "accountability buddies." Here's how to do it.

Choose an initiative that you've been working on or want to start. Write it down here:

_____

_____

_____

_____

Write down five people you could report to about the initiative and why they would be a good choice. Perhaps they are further along than you are in their career, and you can model your success on theirs. Perhaps they are ex-tremely encouraging. Perhaps they are strict and will call you out on your ex-cuses. Choose a variety of people and reasons why they make a good choice. You may want to include social media or a broader group as one of your op-tions.

_____

_____

_____

_____

Choose one or two from your list and write their names here.

_____

_____

_____

_____

Write a plan for how you are going to approach them, what you are committing to, how often you will report your progress to them, and in what manner.

_____

_____

_____

_____

Now do it.

Going Forward

Use this period to hold yourself accountable for your goals and to report to others about your success. Offer to be an accountability buddy to someone striving for a big goal. See if you can find a reciprocal arrangement. Encouraging others to reach their goals and holding them accountable can be a great experience. Seek it out and see how much it can help.

Week 1

1. Power Up with Plants

Placing a plant in your office packs a real punch. Studies have shown that offices with plants have 15% higher productivity because workers are more engaged with their environment. Plants also clean the air, provide noise dampening, and reduce stress. Workers in offices with plants have also been found to take fewer sick days. For a better work environment, go green.

2. Detect and Prevent Misconduct

Which is more important, preventing or detecting misconduct? It used to be that the DOJ guidance focused only on detection. That's no longer true as of the 2023 updates to the Evaluation of Corporate Compliance Program guidance. In two different places, the DOJ added the word "prevent." Programs are no longer made simply to "detect" misconduct, but to "detect and prevent." This may seem like a subtle change, but it's not. If the DOJ comes in, they are likely to focus on what you're doing to prevent misconduct, not just to detect it. Now more than ever, a good compliance program should focus on prevention.

3. Sub-folders Preserve Sanity

Got thousands of emails? Use sub-folders and the archive function to help you to organize your inbox. Move emails as soon as you read them into their correct folder for easy location and retrieval. Once you've started moving emails as a matter of habit, the inbox will magically clear itself.

4. Stop the Wordiness

Before you send a communication, review it for wordiness. Frequently, we use 10 or 12 words where two would suffice. The shorter and punchier you make your sentences, the more easily you will be understood. Complicated sentences may sound impressive in your mind, but for the reader, short and sweet sentences create clear communication.

5. Throw it Out After 30 Days

If you have emails you haven't responded to in 30 days, delete them. Let's face it, if you haven't responded to a message within a month, you're probably not going to. Whatever the issue or question was, it's unlikely to remain relevant now. If the issue was important, you would have likely followed up by now.

The Big Win

This week

_____

_____

_____

_____

_____

_____

_____

I'm Gonna Do It

The tip I've chosen to implement is number _____.

I'm going to implement it by

_____

_____

_____

_____

_____

_____

_____

Week 2

6. Recognize Compliance Champions

Compliance Champions programs have been around for a while, but it's worth noting that the DOJ formally recognized them in their 2023 update to the Evaluation of Corporate Compliance Programs guidance. "Prosecutors should examine whether a company has made working on compliance a means of career advancement, offered opportunities for managers and employees to serve as a compliance champion or made compliance a significant metric for management bonuses." If you haven't yet created a compliance champions program, now is the time.

7. To Be a Good Reporter, Keep Notes in One Place

When you have flashes of insight, do you have a place to write them down? When you hear a great idea at a conference, do you jot it down only to misplace the paper by the end of the event? Try using your phone to record good ideas and keep them in one place. You can use the internal microphone settings, Evernote, WhatsApp, or a notepad app to capture your thoughts. When you're back at your desk, transcribe your notes into a Word document devoted to good ideas. When you're feeling stuck, check that document to keep your good ideas flowing. It'll make all the difference.

8. Ask to Be Removed

Studies have proven that long email chains reduce your cognitive processing. But you probably didn't need a study to tell you that! When you are involved in a long email chain and are no longer necessary to the conversation, ask to be removed. It may seem prudent to remain involved, but every moment taken up by the chain distracts you from productive work. Hedge your bets by asking to be added if you are needed again. The likelihood is that you won't be.

9. Rejection is Redirection

Rejection sucks. It's hard to have your hopes dashed, and it's easy to take rejection personally. Instead of feeling mired in sadness, take a step back and see rejection simply as new information that can help you redirect. Perhaps you need to pivot. Maybe you need to shift your goals or expectations. If you see rejection as providing information to regroup, the sting can be removed, and you can ultimately benefit from it.

10. Stay On Top of Salary Guides

Every couple of years, the Society of Corporate Compliance and Ethics publishes an update to its compliance officer salary survey. Numerous other organizations also publish similar information. Set a Google Alert for "compliance officer salary benchmark" and "compliance officer salary benchmarking." When you're negotiating your pay or next raise, use this tool and others to help you prove your worth.

The Big Win

This week

_____
_____
_____
_____
_____
_____
_____

I'm Gonna Do It

The tip I've chosen to implement is number _____.

I'm going to implement it by

_____
_____
_____
_____
_____
_____
_____

Week 3

11. Keep One Foot in the Past

Your past is valuable, as are the work friendships you made on the job. Aim to be in touch with one person from each company where you've worked. If you're no longer in touch with at least one person, choose a person you liked and reach out on LinkedIn to reconnect. By actively keeping up with your former colleagues, over time, you'll have many people to call on for inspiration when benchmarking your program. You'll also have more friends to turn to when you face a dilemma. After all, that's what friends are for.

12. Set an Inspirational Password

Is your password picking up your spirits? It should be. At a conference, people were asked to name their inspirational passwords. One had "Fee1ingGreatT0day!" while another had "youGotthis!" as hers. Why not give it a try? Change your password to something that makes you feel good. Several times a day you'll reinforce how awesome you are!

13. Visualize the Ratio

If you're running a program at a large company, you likely have regional segregation. When you're looking for a headcount in a particular area, try a simple trick. Visualize the risk of not having a compliance representative in the region by labeling a map with the ratio of compliance officers to employees. If you have, say, 50,000 employees in the APAC region, but no compliance officers, that number is 0/50,000. Just one compliance officer makes the ratio 1/50,000, while two team members bring it to 1/25,000. Visualization can illustrate that you need more of a team!

14. Consider What You Won't Be Doing

If you've asked for additional resources to no avail, be sure to tell your manager or Board what you won't be able to do. Let's say your manager won't fund a new training program. Respond with, "No problem. I just want to make sure you know we'll be sending out the same training as last year, and we won't be able to do the targeted antitrust training, because our current vendor doesn't have antitrust modules available." When people hear what they'll be missing, they'll often rethink their decision. And if they don't, that's fine — you're all on the same page about what to expect.

15. Junk the Junk

If you've subscribed to email lists that don't serve you anymore, don't just delete them. Take the time to unsubscribe. The 30 seconds you spend unsubscribing will give you back many minutes over the course of a year. Get off lists you don't need to free up more time in your day.

The Big Win

This week

_____
_____
_____
_____
_____
_____
_____

I'm Gonna Do It

The tip I've chosen to implement is number ____.
I'm going to implement it by

_____
_____
_____
_____
_____
_____
_____

WEEK 4

16. Expand Your Reading for Inspiration

Reading compliance industry news is important, but it's not enough. Add at least one other type of publication to your reading list, whether that's business news, marketing, sales, data use, or trends in audit. Review new ideas, then challenge yourself to see if they can apply to the compliance program. Learn cutting-edge and cross-functional approaches by expanding your reading horizons.

17. Chop Down Email Chains

When you open your inbox and find 15 emails all with the same subject line, start at the most recent one and read from the bottom. Work all the way up so you can see the whole conversation. From there, open each previous email up and delete any that you've already read in the chain. By doing so, you can quickly work through the whole chain while identifying any email you haven't yet read.

19. Accept or Decline Publicly

Accept, decline, or respond as tentative to meeting requests, and send the requester the response. Some people try to avoid clogging others' inboxes by not sending a response, which sounds thoughtful but can create confusion about who is actually attending. Send the response so people can plan appropriately.

20: Have Your CV at the Ready

Update your CV or resume at least once each year. You never know when a terrific opportunity may come up at the last minute, and you don't want to scramble to put together the document from scratch. Not looking now? By keeping your CV up to date, you'll have a running record of your current accomplishments, which may help you when you go to negotiate a pay raise.

REFLECTION FRIDAY

Use the space below to record any thoughts, feelings, insights, or ideas that arose during the month. You might want to jot down anecdotes from personal relationships, examples from your workday, or anything that you want to internalize and take away from this month.

_____

_____

_____

_____

The Big Win

This week

_____

_____

_____

_____

_____

_____

_____

I'm Gonna Do It

The tip I've chosen to implement is number _____.

I'm going to implement it by

_____

_____

_____

_____

_____

Continuous Improvement

We're now in the last period of Your Year as a Wildly Effective Compliance Officer. It's time to focus on a difficult topic, and that's continuous improvement.

Anyone who has been in the industry knows that the compliance program is never completed. There isn't a finish line. There isn't a victory lap to celebrate completion. Why?

For one, there will always be new laws that require us to shift our programs. There will also be new technologies that will change how we and the business operate. There will be new benchmarks and best practices. Periodically, the risk assessment will be updated, and with it, a new set of mitigating actions assigned.

In addition, opportunities for creating a more ethical company culture come with the territory.

The next training you create can always be more creative or different from those you've given previously.

Mergers and acquisitions will take place. New CEOs will join and change the company's culture and priorities. In short, the compliance program will always be evolving.

Depending on your perspective, that's depressing — or a grand opportunity. If we accept that the program is ongoing, we can forgive ourselves for its imperfections or loose ends. We can give ourselves the grace to keep going when it fails and to commit to the next initiative in the spirit of learning and growth.

Applying the Structure to You

Most compliance officers are success oriented. We were good at school. Most of us went to college, and a majority of us have a law degree, MBA, master's degree, and/or other certifications and qualifications. We're used to finishing the semester and getting a grade, or passing the exam. It's difficult to stare into the void and know that until we die, we'll never really finish. We can choose to stagnate, but even then, the journey isn't over until it's over.

My mother is a big fan of finish lines and competitions. She's always been competitive, and I take after her. Recently, she took up playing the bagpipes — in her 70s. She's joined a band that is slated to go to the world championships in Glasgow next year. Recently, she took first place in a solo competition in Denver. It was her first time as the gold medal winner and I'm certain it won't be the last. In short, she's badass.

About three months into studying aerial arts, my mother asked me what my goal was. The question took me off guard. Is there a goal? Should there be? Is a hobby worth doing if there isn't a finish line? When will I know if I've succeeded?

I'm results-oriented. I want success to be defined. I like checking things off my to-do list. I enjoy feeling accomplished and closing the chapter on an event. But I'm learning to let go of some of that need for a tidy ending.

See, there is no finish line in aerial arts. There isn't a black belt status to achieve. Could I get good enough to perform someday? Maybe. But I'm realistic enough to know I'm never going to be in Cirque du Soleil. Is getting a bit better each week or month enough?

What's my goal? The answer I've come to is this: My goal is continuous improvement. Not to win a competition. Not to be good enough to compete. Not to be as good as Evyn (real name, she's in my school and is amazing to watch). Nope. The goal is to continuously improve and to marvel at my capacity to do so.

My goal is also to appreciate how far I've come instead of comparing myself to how far others have gone. The first time I watched the other girls climb up the silks during class, I couldn't imagine achieving such a feat. Now I climb

20 feet to the ceiling without breaking a sweat. That progress is easy to discount if I'm only focused on the next trick I can't figure out. And trust me, there are many I can't figure out!

We began Q1 by talking about risk assessment. I determined through my personal risk assessment that taking up aerial silks was worth the risk of failure, falling, or the regret of never having tried them. That was a great choice for me, but my journey toward "success" has been harder than I anticipated. Not from a physical perspective. Heck, I knew that would be hard! But from an emotional perspective.

What are you going to continuously improve?

Choosing to be comfortable with continuous improvement can be tough. Think of an area in your life where there isn't a finish line. Write it down:

_____

_____

_____

_____

Next, think about how you've succeeded. This can mean identifying skills you've already learned or milestones you've met. Write those down:

_____

_____

_____

_____

Choose to celebrate those accomplishments. Now commit, in writing, to enjoying the process of continuous improvement.

_____

_____

_____

_____

How will you celebrate your continuous improvement and little suc-cesses?

_____

_____

_____

_____

Going Forward

As we close out the year, think about all the opportunities for continuous improvement. You can improve your relationships, your career, your network, your physical strength, your finances, your aerobic capacity, and your capacity for being in the moment. Every little step forward can yield tremendous positive movement over time.

Week 1

1. Be Present, Stay Connected

When you're giving a presentation or live training, stand at the front of the room and smile at people as they enter. Make eye contact and tell participants that you're excited or grateful that they're there. Your energy is contagious, and people will be intrigued by what you have to say when you start.

2. Step Out of Your Comfort Zone

People tend to avoid situations and experiences that make them uncomfortable. In compliance, however, new rules, regulations, and best practices are simply par for the course. Instead of shying away from a new experience, accept and even embrace the initial discomfort of the inevitable challenges. Acknowledging this will emotionally prepare you for life's inevitable changes — and make you more effective down the line.

3. Sit Front and Center

When you go into a meeting, do you slump to the back of the room and take a seat as far away from the presenter as possible? Do you feel safer not being seen? Instead of hiding in the back, make a conscious choice to sit at the front of the room, preferably facing the door so you can see people enter. Sitting in front signals that you're important and that you belong in the space. You're also more inclined to pay attention and participate, making you an effective audience member who gets noticed.

4. The best is the enemy of the good. — *Voltaire*

Although we all want our work to be terrific, sometimes we need to stop when the work is good enough. It's easy to convince ourselves that everything must be perfect before it's turned in, but those perfectionist tendencies can mean that other projects get pushed or deadlines get missed. When trying to decide if a project is good enough, imagine if your subordinate turned in the same product to you. If you'd be satisfied with the work had someone else produced it, consider yourself done.

5. Thank You in Advance

If you are sending an email requesting an action or a favor, closing with "thank you in advance" is a scientifically proven way to up your chances of a response. This phrase was found to be more effective than best, sincerely, yours truly, and every other variation of the closing. "Thank you in advance" assumes the other person will do what you've asked, which makes them more likely to do it.

The Big Win

This week

_____

_____

_____

_____

_____
_____
_____

I'm Gonna Do It

The tip I've chosen to implement is number _____.

I'm going to implement it by

_____
_____
_____
_____
_____
_____
_____

Week 2:

6. Color Your Screen for Success

Did you know that the color of your screen and the items around you can affect your creativity and attention to detail? A study found that people performed tasks requiring attention to detail much more effectively when their screen had a red background. When people were performing tasks related to creativity and out-of-the-box thinking, blue backgrounds evoked significantly more ideas than red screens. Changing the color of your background screen to increase your aptitude for certain tasks can increase your overall efficacy.

7. Plan a Fake Commute

If you're working from home and feeling burned out, try the fake commute. Having a routine that segregates your home time from your working time reduces stress significantly. Before you start work, go on a quick five to 10-minute walk. Try getting a coffee, then coming inside to work at your desk.

At the end of the day, repeat the behavior by going for a walk after you put away your computer. Your stress level will decrease, and the energy you have to face your day will increase.

8. Working from Home? Go From Sneakers to Slippers

If you work remotely and find it difficult to separate work from home life, you're not alone. Try wearing one pair of shoes "to the office" and changing out of them at the end of your workday. If you're American, you probably know that Mr. Rogers, the children's TV presenter, comes home from work, takes off his blazer, and puts on his cardigan in the show's opening credits. That same trick works for home office workers, too. Changing your shoes will shift your mindset, allowing you to come home emotionally at the end of the day.

9. Disconnect for Greater Success

Have you ever thought that were it not for email, you could get so much more done? Why not take it one step further and disconnect for a few minutes, or even hours, at a time? Just click off your Wi-Fi or unplug your ethernet cable. Yes, it will feel weird at first. However, your focused periods will be super productive. If you're worried, put a meeting on your calendar. You do have a meeting: a date with your more productive self.

10. Make Your Home Office Inspiring

If you only work from home occasionally, you might think that the appearance of your desk doesn't matter. After all, no one at work will see it. But that's no reason to settle for clutter or sparseness. Instead, pick two or three items that bring you joy. Inspiring quotes, a beautiful calendar, pictures of your loved ones, or any other objects that remind you why you're working are good options. Everyone appreciates a well-organized environment, so making your home office (or dining room table) aesthetically pleasing will foster creativity and speed up the day. It'll simply make you happier, too.

The Big Win

This week

_____
_____
_____
_____
_____
_____
_____
_____

I'm Gonna Do It

The tip I've chosen to implement is number _____.

I'm going to implement it by

_____
_____
_____
_____
_____
_____
_____

Week 3

11. Start Constructive Criticism with a Specific Complement

Nobody enjoys receiving negative feedback. It's a struggle for both the person offering criticism and the person on the receiving end. When you must give constructive criticism, start with an example of a time when the person got it right (or close to right), and then follow with your feedback. For instance, if you sat in on an investigatory interview where your direct report asked mostly softball questions, find one really good question, and tell them to come up with more like it. Starting with the positive will make your direct report more open to the feedback, and help them connect it to familiar concepts.

12. Make Meetings 15 or 20

Most meetings are scheduled for 30 minutes or an hour, but instead of scheduling meetings for these default times, think about the time you actually need. If you think you only need 15 minutes, schedule for 15. If you think you need 20 minutes, schedule for 20. By scheduling shorter meetings, you'll signal to others that you mean business and that you intend to take care of it in the allotted time. Instead of scheduling 30 minutes, and then "having 10 minutes back for your day," only schedule 20 to begin with. You'll save time and set clear expectations.

13. Be Regular

Schedule regular check-ins with every important stakeholder. Whether it's the president of your region, the CEO, or head of sales, by having regular check-ins, you are more likely to build relationships. Getting leaders used to talking to you, sharing information, and sharing strategy is critical to building trust. The more they trust you with regular conversations, the more likely they are to come to you when they have questions or things are difficult.

14. Think Globally

Want to move abroad? Then become the go-to person on international laws and trends. Data privacy laws are more stringent outside of the United States, sanctions are at an all-time high, and anti-money laundering regulatory regimes updating constantly. By getting up to speed on international laws affecting compliance, you can speak about them in detail and discuss the trends with potential employers, making you an attractive candidate who is likely to get the job.

15. "Can I Get Your Perspective?"

Sometimes, we need help to complete a project. Other times, we need to let our boss know a project can't be done in time. Instead of going to your boss in frustration with your hands thrown up, ask for their perspective. Let's say you've been working hard on a project for weeks, and your deadline is in two days. You could enlist a coworker, but you feel uncomfortable asking directly. Try saying to your boss, "I'd love your perspective on this. I'm working diligently to complete the project, and I'm almost there, but help would be great. What are your thoughts?" Your boss will likely be flattered, and it may get the desired result without making a direct request.

The Big Win

This week

_____

_____

_____

_____

_____

_____

_____

I'm Gonna Do It

The tip I've chosen to implement is number ____.

I'm going to implement it by

_____

_____

_____

_____

_____

_____

_____

Week 3

16. Make Hot-Desking Less Horrible

If you've been called back to the office, it's possible that you're hot-desking, or being assigned a desk based on a rotating system due to lack of availability. In The New York Times, a piece about making hot-desking less awful offered tips such as "neighborhooding", or demarcating certain areas for teams. Instead of searching throughout the open space for a desk near your colleagues, an area would be designated for the legal and compliance team. Having a dedicated area allows you to interact with your colleagues, and mitigates the frustration of trying to find a new seat every time. If you're not neighborhooding, suggest it to management as a way to boost efficiency and morale.

17. Don't Be Defensive

Although it can be difficult, when someone is critical of you or the compliance program, do your best to listen to the feedback. Most people become defensive when feedback is offered, which stops their capacity to learn. Unemotionally evaluate whether the feedback is useful. If it is, make changes to make it better.

18. Stash Your Cell Phone

When you're having a face-to-face conversation, stash your cell phone out of view, unless you have an emergency or are actively awaiting a specific email. People like to feel that they are important, and there is nothing like dedicated, single-focus attention to make others feel safe. Keep the cell phone away, information will flow, and camaraderie will come faster.

19. Stop the Uncertainty

Humans detest uncertainty. Studies have shown that people are much better at dealing with bad news than waiting to find out if something bad has happened. We can make life better for our employees by ending uncertainty as quickly as we can. If you've come to a conclusion after an investigation, share the outcome as soon as possible. If you know that a new initiative won't pass legal muster, tell them quickly. They'll be thankful for your humanity, even if they don't like the outcome.

20. Stop the Pre-Suffering

Are you guilty of "pre-suffering?" It's common, but it's not a good use of your time or energy. While it is useful to have a contingency plan if things go wrong, ruminating on negative outcomes puts your body in fight or flight mode, causing you to repeatedly suffer the negative event when nothing has happened. The antidote is to remind yourself that you're strong enough to overcome anything bad that happens. If things do go wrong, you'll deal with it in the moment. Don't suffer before you need to — especially since you might not need to suffer at all.

REFLECTION FRIDAY

Use the space below to record any thoughts, feelings, insights, or ideas that arose during the month. You might want to jot down anecdotes from personal relationships, examples from your workday, or anything that you want to internalize and take away from this month.

_____

_____

_____

_____

The Big Win

This week

_____

_____

_____

_____

_____

_____

_____

I'm Gonna Do It

The tip I've chosen to implement is number _____.

I'm going to implement it by

_____

_____

_____

_____

_____

_____

_____

Your Quarterly Audit

t's time to reflect on the four tips you chose to implement. This evaluation is important because the repetitive acknowledgment of your goals and actions keeps you on track.

Part 1: EVALUATION

Directions: Write the number of each tip you implemented, and check each box that applies. Some tips might apply across the board, while others only relate to one category.

Tip. No.	Completed Tip	Lead to greater work success	Improved my non-work life	Both

Part 2: REFLECTION

1. Which tips will you carry through to the next quarter?

_____

_____

_____

2. Which tips influence your mental space? (positive thinking, achieve-ment, and goal setting)

_____

_____

_____

3. Which tips changed your physical space? (Your home office, at-work desk, etc.)

_____

_____

_____

4. Which tips came naturally to you, and which forced you to step out of your comfort zone?

_____

_____

_____

5. Which is/are part of a larger push toward improvement in one area of your life?

_____

_____

_____

6.   Which revealed existing strengths, and which showed areas of improvement? Weaknesses?

_____

_____

_____

7.   *Bonus*: Which one are you going to share with others?

_____

_____

_____

Your Adventure Continues

Congratulations on completing your year as a Wildly Effective Compliance Officer!

During this year, you've accomplished some great things.

In Q1, you assessed the risk of missing out on the life you love and made shifts accordingly. You examined the policies (or rules) you unconsciously chose for your life and decided whether or not they served you. You made a plan to bring more joy and fulfillment into your life.

In Q2, you identified people who are hard to communicate with, then shifted your style to make it easier to interact with them. You determined areas where discipline would help you to achieve your goals. You also examined the meetings, people, and activities taking up your time, and chose which to keep and which to ditch.

In Q3, you created a plan to keep stretching and learning through training in educational or physical pursuits. You identified areas of malaise or dis-ease, and performed an internal investigation to find the root cause. You also identified situations where kinder self-talk and incentives for your good behavior might improve your life.

In Q4, you monitored activities and metrics to keep you on track toward your goals. You accelerated your progress by using an accountability strategy like an accountability buddy or going public with your objectives. You accepted the reality of continuous improvement, and are committed to incrementally improving over time.

In short, you've done a heck of a lot!

Using Your Big Wins

In addition, you've got your Big Wins list. This list is so important. Looking back over it should make you grin. You've done more than you ever realized.

You can use your big list in a number of ways. First, identify your biggest work successes and use them to guide your annual evaluation. People frequently forget their Q1 accomplishments. Use the whole year's list to show your successes. It's easier to make the case for a raise or promotion when pointing to a pile of accomplishments.

Next, identify your biggest emotional or personal wins. At work, you may have built a positive relationship with a difficult boss or co-worker. Maybe you became a better presenter/trainer, or learned a new area of compliance law. You can use the pages at the end of this book to create these lists.

When you're feeling down or like nothing is going your way, take out your Big Wins list to reinforce your greatness. It will lift your spirits.

I'm Gonna Do It List

Over the course of the year, you chose 48 tips to implement and planned how you'd apply them. You then conducted quarterly audits to assess your progress. Hopefully, you've found several tips that have made a profound difference in propelling you forward as a Wildly Effective Compliance Officer.

Look back at your quarterly audits and decide which tips you'll carry with you in the next year. Write down at least five — preferably ten. You can use the pages at the end of this book to create this list.

If You Finished the Book in Less than a Year

If you've finished reading the book in less than a year, great! Continue to write down your big wins every week so you're ready for your performance review, and choose those tips to implement on a weekly basis. It's worth it to complete those exercises over the course of a year, as new habits take time to solidify.

What to Do Next

There's no reason not to have another year as a Wildly Effective Compliance Officer. Throughout the upcoming year, go back and revisit the tips. Choose different tips to implement so that you experience their full power to transform you into a more effective professional. You'll have nearly 100 new habits in two years!

Dip into the book when you need inspiration or a solution to a tough work problem. Know that the answers you need are never far away. Believe that the right tip will come at the right time. And more than anything...

Never Forget the Meaning Behind Our Work

I believe with my whole soul that what we do as compliance officers is changing how business is done, and you, as a compliance professional, are genuinely changing the world.

It's easy to get caught up in the day-to-day minutiae of our job. Writing a policy, giving a training session, or creating slides for a board report doesn't always feel rewarding or meaningful. The job can be monotonous, defeating, lonely, depressing, and uncomfortable. You may feel ignored or even despised. You may feel like you're pushing sand uphill all day long, not achieving anything. You're not alone. Most of us feel that way sometimes.

When it doesn't seem worth it, remember that you are an essential part of the movement that is changing the world for the better. The African Union estimates that $140 billion is lost to corruption each year. To put that number in perspective, that amount could ensure uninterrupted power 24 hours a day to every citizen in Africa for three years. Your anti-bribery work curtails corruption, if only through the power of organizations not normalizing bribery and preventing it from happening where you work.

When you stop your company from doing business with a sanctioned third-party, you halt the flow of money to terrorism, gangs, human traffickers, and other forms of criminality. When you teach your salespeople to avoid price fixing, you make the playing field fair for new entrepreneurs to bring game-changing products to market. They may create new jobs, spark innovation, and improve people's lives.

When you perform modern slavery reviews or human impact assessments, you focus attention on the most vulnerable members of society and ensure your company is doing the right thing to protect them.

You really are changing the world, one ethical corporate action at a time.

Our Work Is Never Done

Compliance will never be finished. Eventually, we will all stop working, whether in the profession or in general. But compliance will never be done. And that's a good thing.

Corporations will always need people who steward them toward ethical choices. New laws will require new responses. New technologies and new business practices will demand scrutiny and guardrails. We're here for that.

You could equate this with job security, and for most of us, it does guarantee work. While any one job may not be secure forever, the profession as a whole isn't going anywhere. It will evolve and change, but corporations will always need help in complying with the law, performing internal investigations, training employees, creating policies, and reporting about compliance and ethical behavior to the executives and the Board.

As the world continues to awaken to the importance of ethical business, now is a brilliant time to be a compliance officer. And an even better time to be a Wildly Effective one.

You Are a Hero

The compliance profession has many unsung heroes who are changing the world for the better every day. You stand among them, and for that, I am deeply grateful.

Thank you for embarking on this journey to become an even more Wildly Effective Compliance Officer. I am proud to be with you on this march toward a better world.

Let's keep going — together.

Acknowledgements

Writing this book has been a true joy. Many thanks to my brilliant editor and collaborator, Alizah Salario. Your insights and clarity made this book what it is.

Thank you to my stellar husband, Jonathan Grant-Hart, for his enormous contributions to my life and his willingness to allow pieces of our story and his life to be included in this manuscript. You are truly the one in whom my soul delights.

Thank you also to my courageous and charismatic mother, Kathy Elwood. Your stories shine brightly in this book because of your grit, love, and passion. I appreciate you so much.

To my father, Kerry S. Grant, whose presence in my life inspired me to reach for new heights. I hope you can see how far I've come since your passing. You're always in my heart.

To my sisters, Kelly and Kimberly, to whom this book is dedicated. You two are the most remarkable women. I am so grateful to have you in my life.

To my beautiful niece Delilah – may your life benefit from the trailblazers before you, especially the many women of courage in this profession.

And to my family – my feisty and fabulous nephew Grant, Linda, the Grants, Woods, Blacks, Harts, and Elwoods.

To all of the Sparkies, past and present. In the beginning, I could never imagine the talent I would have working around me every day. I appreciate you more than I could ever put into words. Thank you for helping to realize my vision for Spark Compliance. It's an amazing thing to watch it grow. I stand in awe, knowing I could never build this without you.

To my friends who make my life so much fun. To Lisa, Megan, Chris, Marnie, Natalie, Chris V.E., and Michele – I love you all.

To the incredible compliance community – you've taught me every day. Special thanks to the wonderful Tom Fox, my podcasting partner and friend. And to Joe Murphy, who believed in me early and supported my dreams in such a potent way. Many thanks also to Kirsten Liston, Richard Bistrong, Mary Shirley, Matt Kelly, and Carrie Penman. I appreciate you so much.

Writing a book that is years in the making means that there are more people to thank than I could ever mention here. To everyone who has inspired me, taught me, written books that I loved and learned from, forged pathways for me, mentored or sponsored me...thank you.

ABOUT THE AUTHOR

Kristy Grant-Hart is an expert in designing and implementing effective international compliance programs for multi-national companies. She is a professional speaker, author, former professor, and thought leader in the compliance profession. She is the founder and CEO of Spark Compliance Consulting, an international consulting company specializing in pragmatic, proportionate, and pro-business compliance and ethics solutions. She is also the creator of the Compliance Competitor game and other compliance-related software and training products.

Mrs. Grant-Hart formerly served as Chief Compliance Officer for United International Pictures, the joint distribution company for Paramount Pictures and Universal Pictures, based in London. While there, she was shortlisted for the Chief Compliance Officer of the Year award at the Women in Compliance Awards.

Mrs. Grant-Hart was an Adjunct Professor at Delaware School of Law, Widener University teaching Global Compliance and Ethics to Masters of Jurisprudence students. Mrs. Grant-Hart began her legal career at the international law firm of Gibson, Dunn & Crutcher, where she worked in the firm's Los Angeles and London offices.

Mrs. Grant-Hart graduated summa cum laude from Loyola Law School in California. She holds certification as a Corporate Compliance and Ethics Professional – International (CCEP-I) and is a member of the California Bar.

She lives in California with her husband Jonathan and beloved rescue dog, Mr. Fox.

Made in United States
North Haven, CT
25 March 2024

50472222R00117